OXFORD PSYCHOLOGY SERIES

Editors

Nicholas J. Mackintosh   Anne Treisman
Daniel Schacter   Lawrence Weiskrantz
Timothy Shallice

*Understanding
Figurative
Language*

Understanding Figurative Language

FROM METAPHORS TO IDIOMS

Sam Glucksberg

with a contribution by
Matthew S. McGlone

OXFORD PSYCHOLOGY SERIES
NUMBER 36

OXFORD
UNIVERSITY PRESS
2001

OXFORD

UNIVERSITY PRESS

Oxford New York
Athens Auckland Bangkok Bogotá Buenos Aires Calcutta
Cape Town Chennai Dar es Salaam Delhi Florence Hong Kong Istanbul
Karachi Kuala Lumpur Madrid Melbourne Mexico City Mumbai Nairobi
Paris São Paulo Shanghai Singapore Taipei Tokyo Toronto Warsaw

and associated companies in
Berlin Ibadan

Published by Oxford University Press, Inc.
198 Madison Avenue, New York, New York 10016

Library of Congress Cataloging-in-Publication Data
Glucksberg, Sam.
    Understanding figurative language : from metaphors to idioms / Sam Glucksberg ;
with a contribution by Matthew S. McGlone.
    p. cm.—(Oxford psychology series ; no. 36)
Includes bibliographical references and index.
ISBN-13 978-0-19-511109-5
ISBN 0-19-511109-5
1. Figures of speech. I. McGlone, Matthew S., 1966– II. Title. III. Series.
P301 .G56 2000
808—dc21   00-025745

9 8 7 6 5 4 3 2

Printed in the United States of America
on acid-free paper

Preface

How do people understand utterances that are intended figuratively? In figurative language, the intended meaning does not coincide with the literal meanings of the words and sentences that are used. In metaphor, for example, literal meaning is often patently absurd, as in "New York may be the next Orange County." In idioms, the relation between literal meaning and idiomatic meaning may be totally opaque, as in *kicked the bucket* or *bought the farm*. Both of these idiomatic phrases mean "died," but people have no idea of how or why these idioms have come to mean what they do.

Traditionally, figurative language such as metaphors and idioms has been considered derivative from and more complex than ostensibly straightforward literal language. A contemporary view, as exemplified not only in psychological but also in linguistic and philosophical research, is that figurative language involves the same kinds of linguistic and pragmatic operations that are used for ordinary, literal language. Put another way, we can identify two sets of operations that people use in comprehending discourse. One set consists of purely linguistic operations, such as lexical access, syntactic analysis, and so forth. A second set consists of a less well-defined grab-bag of operations, usually grouped under the term *pragmatics*. Whatever the utility of this distinction, so-called literal language requires the full use of both kinds of operations, no less and perhaps no different than that required for figurative language.

Over the past decade my colleagues and I have studied how people use and understand metaphor and idioms. We have focused exclusively on ordinary language, expressions that are used in daily life, including conversations about everyday matters and that appear in newspapers, magazines, and other media. We have explicitly excluded the more complex uses of figurative language in poetry, fiction, or other forms of creative writing. We have also excluded consideration of metaphor's intricate and central roles in culture and society. We believe that our approach and theories do apply to these more complex metaphor contexts and uses, but it is crystal clear that the theories are vastly insufficient. With respect to daily conversational discourse, we have developed a theoretical account of how figurative expressions are understood and have tested our theories with an extensive body of experimental research. Most of our work has been devoted to metaphor, and so metaphor is the major focus of the book. Idioms, however, are also treated comprehensively and in reasonable detail.

The book begins with a consideration of metaphor and other kinds of tropes. I consider linguistic, philosophical, and psychological approaches to the study of language and how each of these three disciplines sets the issues and problems. In particular, I examine and evaluate how each has dealt with the special problem of figurative language. The central issue for this chapter is the assumption that literal meaning is primary and central to language use and comprehension. In chapter 2, this assumption is challenged on both theoretical and empirical grounds.

Chapter 3 addresses the role of comparison processes in metaphor comprehension, the creation of new categories via metaphor, and the strategies that people use to name new, nonlexicalized categories. In this chapter I argue that metaphor comprehension involves property attribution, not comparison. I also introduce the notion of dual reference, whereby metaphors such as *jail* in the expression "my job is a *jail*" can be used to refer to the literal jail and at the same time to the more abstract category of things and situations that the literal jail can epitomize: things or situations that are punishing, confining, unpleasant, and so on. In chapter 4, I review the experimental evidence in support of the property-attribution and dual-reference views, with particular attention to those studies that discriminate between comparison and attribution models of metaphor comprehension.

In chapter 5 I analyze idioms and the relationships between metaphor and idiom. I argue that idioms do not consist of a single type of expression but instead vary systematically from simple phrases such as *by and large*, to metaphors, albeit frozen ones, in their own right, as in *bury the hatchet*. I propose a taxonomy of idioms and report a series of studies that show how people integrate word meanings, idiomatic meanings, and social/cultural knowledge to produce and to understand idiomatic expressions. I also discuss the reasons that idioms pose particular problems for people learning second languages, and the problem of translating idioms from one language to another.

Chapter 6, contributed by Matthew McGlone, critically examines the conceptual metaphor theory proposed by Lakoff and his colleagues. Lakoff argues that all human conceptualization is based on metaphor and that deep conceptual metaphors are used to understand figurative expressions in daily discourse. McGlone argues against this view on both theoretical and empirical grounds, showing that metaphors and idioms can be understood at several levels of analysis and also indicating the circumstances in which people use deep conceptual metaphors and, more important, when they do not.

Throughout my work on figurative language, I have enjoyed the support of and inspiration from a wonderful group of students and colleagues. Among the students who have become close friends and colleagues are Boaz Keysar, Matthew McGlone, Roger Kreuz, Sachi Kumon Nakamura, Mary Newsome, Yevgeniya Goldvarg, and Zachary Estes. I am particularly grateful to Cristina Cacciari, who first aroused my interest in idioms, and to Mary Engel, with whom I am now studying how second-language learners cope with American English idioms. These colleagues, as well as Rachel Giora, Josef Stern, and an anonymous reviewer, provided helpful and insightful comments on earlier drafts of the manuscript. I am also grateful to the support provided by the National Institutes of Health and to the National Science Foundation for their generous support of my research. I am indebted to the Center for Advanced Study in the Behavioral Sciences, where I spent the 1986–87 academic year as a resident Fellow. In addition to giving me the opportunity to improve my volleyball game, the Institute gave me the space, time, and stimulation I needed to begin my foray into figurative language studies. Finally, I thank my wife, Kay Deaux, for her critical and wise reading of the earlier drafts of the book. She has been an unwavering source of encouragement, wisdom, and delight.

May 2000   S. G.
Princeton, New Jersey

Contents

Understanding
Figurative
Language

Metaphor

The Central Trope

The metaphor is probably the most fertile power possessed by man.
Jose Ortega y Gasset, 1948

The word *metaphor* derives from the Greek *metapherein*, transfer, as META= + *pherein*, to bear (*Oxford English Dictionary*, 1996). From this deceptively simple root, metaphor has come to mean different things to different people, so much so that specialists in the area are often temporarily confounded when asked for a definition of *metaphor*. I vividly recall (with some amusement) an incident in which an esteemed colleague and occasional theoretical adversary, Ray Gibbs,[1] was being interviewed by Israeli security personnel during check-in for a flight to Tel Aviv. When asked why he was flying to Tel Aviv, Gibbs replied that he had been invited to a conference on metaphor. The interviewer asked, "What's a metaphor?" When Gibbs hesitated, momentarily at a loss for words, the interviewer asked sharply, "You're going to a metaphor conference and you don't even know what a metaphor is?" A consternated Professor Gibbs was thereupon hustled away by security guards and interrogated for almost an hour before one of the conference hosts, an Israeli professor from the University of Tel Aviv, intervened and vouched for Ray's legitimacy, if not for his quickness of tongue.

Metaphor challenges definition for at least two reasons.[2] First, the term is used in several different, albeit related, senses. Second, both within and between its different senses, definitions vary to reflect sharply different theoretical agendas and assumptions. Sometimes the theoretical boundaries coincide with scholarly disciplines; thus, philosophers; linguists, and psychologists might each define metaphor in their own terms. But there are

3

differences even within disciplines that reflect different views of metaphor, as well as different views of the nature of language itself.

Dictionary entries for the term *metaphor* provide illustrative examples of how metaphor can be variously defined. The two major senses of the term are captured in the *Oxford English Dictionary* (1996). The first sense identifies metaphor as a type of language: "A figure of speech in which a name or descriptive word or phrase is transferred to an object or action different from, but analogous to, that to which it is literally applicable; an instance of this [is] a metaphorical expression." The second sense identifies metaphor as a form of conceptual representation: "A thing considered as representative of some other (usually abstract) thing: A symbol."

A particular instance of metaphor use can illustrate both of these senses simultaneously, as when crime is referred to in terms of disease: "Crime in our city has become an epidemic that will soon infect even our finest neighborhoods." In this instance, one thing, *crime*, is considered as a representative instance of some other thing, *disease*. The concept *disease* is thus used as a metaphor for the concept *crime*. If we can conceptualize crime as an instance of disease, then crime can have (at least some of) the properties of diseases: it can be infectious, it can be endemic, it can be an epidemic, we might try to "cure" it, there might even be a crime virus. And, if crime can have properties of diseases, then we can use the vocabulary of disease to talk about crime, as in *He's been cured of his thieving ways*, or *Corruption and bribery are a cancer in the body politic*. Lehrer (1978) provides a detailed analysis of how a conceptual relationship is first expressed in terms of a root metaphor—for example, *Personalities are like textures*—and then expanded via novel instantiations of this metaphor, as in *George is rough around the edges*. Theories of metaphor in philosophy, linguistics, and psychology, as well as in anthropology and sociology, address one or more aspects of these two senses of metaphor: metaphor as a form of linguistic expression and communication and metaphor as a form of conceptual representation and symbolization. Analogously, literary theory and criticism also address the issues of metaphor in these two senses, metaphor as literary or poetic device and metaphor as symbol. Most often, the two senses are treated as if they were independent of each other, with Lakoff and his colleagues (Lakoff & Johnson, 1980; Lakoff & Turner, 1989) a notable exception. We return to this issue in chapter 6. For now, we briefly consider metaphor as linguistic expression.

Metaphor as Substitution

In the *Poetics* (chapter 21), Aristotle proposed four types of metaphors: genus for genus, genus for species, species for genus, and analogy. The first three types share a common characteristic: the substitution of one word for another.[3] Genus-for-genus metaphors have received the most attention in contemporary treatments of metaphor, where they are usually referred to as nominal metaphors and predicative metaphors. Nominal metaphors substitute, in Aristotle's terms, one noun for another, as in *some lawyers are sharks*. The metaphor vehicle, *sharks*, is used instead of a word that belongs to the same genus—that is, category or semantic domain—as the metaphor topic, *some lawyers*.[4] A serious difficulty with the substitution notion is immediately apparent. The noun *shark* presumably substitutes for some other noun that is in the same semantic domain as "some lawyers," but what is substituted for what is unclear: what noun might that be? Similarly, in predicative metaphors, verbs are said to be substituted for one another, as in *the guard dog flew across the backyard to challenge the intruder*. Dogs cannot literally fly, but the verb *flew* substitutes for some other verb that could literally denote an action that dogs can perform. However, as in the nominal case, what might that other verb be?

Substitution is not as problematic in the two types of metonymy in which genus substitutes for species or species substitutes for genus.[5] In these expressions, the two terms are drawn from the same semantic domain, and the substitution involves level of specificity, rather than semantic domain.[6] Using a more general term such as *insect* to refer to cockroaches, as in *the insects scurried when she switched on the kitchen light*, would technically be considered a genus-for-species metaphor. In expressions that substitute genus for species or species for genus, what substitutes for what is clear. A more general term, such as *insect*, can substitute for a more specific term, such as *tick*, which in turn can substitute for a still more specific term, *deer tick*. However, it may be inappropriate to refer to such expressions as metaphors, or even as instances of substitution per se. Whenever we make reference, we choose a level of specificity that is appropriate in context. What principles govern such choices?

At the most general level, I assume that people follow Grice's (1975) cooperative principle. When speaking, people implicitly cooperate with one another in order to further the purposes of their conversation (see also Clark, 1996, for an extended analysis of conversation as a collaborative activity). In order to be cooperative, people try to be relevant, truthful, clear and informative. A speaker's choice of level of specificity should be guided by this consideration. For example, if I need change for a soda machine, I would not ask my companion for a 1989 quarter, nor would I simply ask for a coin. The former is overly specific, the latter too general. The appropriate level of specificity in the context would identify the coin or coins that I need for the soda machine—a quarter if that's what I need, a dime or a nickel if these are the coins that I need.

What governs the default level of specificity? The default level of referring expressions is usually at the basic level of categorization. Anything can be referred to at various levels of specificity. A piano can be referred to at the superordinate level, *musical instrument*, at the subordinate level, *grand piano*, or at an intermediate level, *piano*. The intermediate level is commonly known as the basic level (Rosch, 1973, 1978), a level that usually suffices for conversational reference that is neither overly general nor overly specific. The basic level can thus be characterized as the level of usual utility (Brown, 1958a), which usually becomes the default level of specificity. Unless a context indicates otherwise, people use the default (usual) level of specificity, which in most cases is the basic level. If a more specific or more general level would be more informative, then speakers should choose accordingly. For someone in need of a quarter for a soda machine, the basic level "coin" would be inappropriate: "quarter" would be the appropriate choice. For a panhandler on a street corner, *some change* would be the most appropriate. *Money* would be too general, *nickels, dimes*, or *quarters* too specific. These examples illustrate systematic and contextually appropriate departures from Brown's level of "usual" utility. Viewed in this light, substitution of genus for species and vice versa is a choice of level of specificity, not a choice to use figurative instead of literal language. Substitutions of superordinate for subordinate and the reverse, while technically instances of metonymy, are best characterized as ordinary literal language, albeit tailored to suit particular situations.

Other types of metonymic substitutions seem more figurative, as when a part of something is used to refer to the whole, for example, *wheels* to refer to automobiles, as in *she's really proud of her new wheels*. These types of metonymy do not involve substitutions between levels of specificity but instead substitute a term that is associated in one or another way with the intended referent. In such expressions, places can refer to their occupants, as in *The White House is stonewalling the special prosecutor*; an object can refer to its user, as in *the glove at shortstop made two errors in yesterday's game*; a part can refer to a whole, as in *the bigmouth went down in the first round*. As Turner (1987) points out, an expression may be used to refer to anything that it is conventionally associated with. Thus, people's names can be used to refer to their works, as in *I read Jane Austen every night before bedtime* or *Harry bought another Hockney last week*. The constraints on such referring expressions seem to be primarily cultural and often depend on the relative distinctiveness of the association. Thus, I could say that *I love Sarah Lee* to mean that I love the cakes that are sold under that name. However, I could not felicitously refer to a steak grilled by my friend Bob as *I love Bob* (Gibbs, 1993). In addition to culturally shared associations, specific contexts can enable metonymic reference, as when a waiter in a restaurant says that *the lobster will be having white wine tonight* to refer to a customer who had ordered lobster (Nunberg, 1979). But these latter kinds of usages, as in the levels-of-specificity substitutions, don't seem to be metaphoric or figurative at all. What kinds of metonymies function as metaphors?

One possibility is that metonymic expressions function as metaphors when they involve transference, in the original Greek sense of the term. One form of such metonymic transference is a bridging or mapping between the abstract and the concrete (Gibbs, 1994), as in such substitutions as *bench* for *the law, car bomb* for *terrorism, pen* for *writer*, and *oval office* for *the presidency*. Another form of transference conveys or emphasizes a salient characteristic of the referent by substituting that characteristic for the referent itself, as in *kitchen* for *chef, arm* for *baseball pitcher, skirt* for *young woman*, and *lip* for a *brash, talkative person*. When, however, a referring expression functions solely to identify an entity and nothing more, then it is not considered metaphoric. The restaurant practice of referring to patrons in terms of their orders (e.g., the *hamburger* wants a Coke) functions in this way, identifying a referent without characterizing it in any way.

Some Problems with the Concept of Substitution

The nature of substitutions in metonymic expressions is, as we have seen, clear and unproblematic. However, the metaphoric status of such expressions is not quite so clear and unproblematic. In the most important of tropes, genus-for-genus metaphors, metaphoric status is not at issue, but the nature of the putative substitution is. Following Gibbs (1994), I will use the term *metaphor* in its narrow sense to refer to expressions that involve two conceptual domains and metonymy to those that involve just one (see note 6).

Metaphors pose a thorny problem for the substitution view. In expressions such as *man is a wolf*, what word does *wolf* substitute for? According to the substitution view, the metaphor resides in replacing a literal expression with the metaphorical *wolf*. But there does not seem to be any way to transform the metaphor into a literal statement by replacing *wolf* with a literal equivalent. The obvious reason is that there is no literal equivalent of *wolf* in this context, certainly not a single-word equivalent. If there were, then there would be no reason to use a metaphor rather than a literal expression.

What, then, is the nature of the substitution in metaphors, particularly metaphors of the form X is Y, where X and Y are from different conceptual domains? The substitution seems more an implicit act than a concrete substitution such as we have seen in metonymic expressions. The substitution argument does not seem to go beyond the claim that a metaphor vehicle such as *wolf* substitutes, in some unspecified way, for a term or terms from the same semantic domain as the topic, *man*. Alternatively, the substitution could be taken to refer to any literal paraphrase of the metaphor vehicle, so that *wolf* might substitute for a literal rendering of the metaphor ground. In the metaphor *man is a wolf*, *wolf* substitutes for something like "a predatory creature, stealthy and vicious, with fierce loyalties to the pack (read family, group, country, gang, etc.), etc. . . ." The *etc.* here is the rub, as is the open-ended nature of the literal paraphrase of the ground. There is no single, definitive interpretation to be given of this or any other nontrivial metaphor. Metaphor interpretations are constructed from the meanings of the two metaphor terms, topic and vehicle, often with the context of the conversation playing an important role. For example, *elephant* in Western society can serve either as a symbol of enormous size or as a symbol of prodigious memory. The metaphor *David is an elephant* can thus be taken to mean either that David is a very large man or that he has a prodigious memory. Does the phrase "is an elephant" substitute for "is a very large man" or "has a prodigious memory," or does it instead provide these characterizations as possible attributes of David?

Because of the insoluble problem of specifying exactly what is substituted for what in metaphor, the strong form of the substitution view has sunk into oblivion, but not without leaving a significant trace. Its basic assumptions survive, recast in terms of standard pragmatic theory. These assumptions include:

1. Literal meaning is basic and has unconditional priority. Implicit in this assumption is a corollary assumption: that literal meaning is unproblematic and is context-free, that is, the literal meanings of expressions remain unchanged regardless of context of use.

2. Figurative meaning is derived from the literal and can be discovered by discovering the nature of the substitution of the metaphorical for the literal. One implication of this assumption is that metaphoric interpretations involve recovering the original literal expression for which the metaphor substitutes.

3. It follows from assumptions 1 and 2 that metaphor understanding is more complex and requires more cognitive work than literal understanding. Metaphor understanding also requires the use of contextual information, which literal understanding, by definition, does not.

For these reasons, among others, many linguists and philosophers of language take the position that metaphor lies outside theories of meaning or semantics. Linguists are concerned with the relations between form and meaning, that is, the meanings of individual words and the meanings of sentences that can be derived compositionally, that is, by rule, from the meanings of the sentence constituents. When the meaning of an utterance cannot be specified in purely linguistic terms, then that kind of meaning is simply excluded from consideration. Sadock exemplifies this view: "All nonliteral speech . . . including metaphor, falls outside of the domain of synchronic linguistics . . ." (Sadock, 1993, p. 42). Philosophers of language have traditionally been concerned with the truth conditions for expressions. In their view, to know the meaning of an expression is to know the conditions under which that expression would be true or false. Thus, Davidson (1977), for example, emphatically denies that metaphors have a metaphorical meaning over and above their literal meaning: "metaphors mean what the words, in their most literal sense, mean and nothing more" (p. 246). For Davidson, literal meaning is linguistic meaning: it is independent of context, completely systematic and rule governed. Utterances are understood by interpretation, roughly, by first arriving at the literal meaning of an utterance and then by inferring what that literal meaning is used for. If I say *it will rain tomorrow*, there is only one literal meaning, and that meaning is the first one to be derived by an interpreter. The interpreter can, however, infer (in principle) an infinite number of alternate interpretations. I may use the utterance to convey my belief that a particular weather forecast is wrong, or that we should not plan on going to the beach, or that the crops won't fail after all because the drought will end tomorrow, ad infinitum. These and all other possible interpretations of my use of the utterance *it will rain tomorrow* are not alternative meanings but, rather, alternative uses.

The distinctions among form, meaning, and use are motivated by a commitment to language as a logical system, and that meaning resides in truth conditions. To know the meaning of a sentence, on this classical view, is to know the circumstances under which it would be true or false (Miller & Glucksberg, 1988). Thus, to know the meaning of "rain is dry" requires not a belief that the statement is true or false but simply an understanding of the conditions, in all possible worlds, under which the statement would be true or false.[7] More generally, language is a system of learned conventions and regularities that enable literal meanings to be derived independent of context or occasion of utterance. Once literal meanings are derived, then the work of interpretation can begin.[8]

The distinction between meaning and use in truth-conditional semantics is analogous to the distinction between sentence meaning and utterance meaning in standard pragmatic theory. As initially proposed by Grice (1975), there are at least two kinds of logic involved in discourse comprehension: the logic of language and the logic of conversation. The logic of language applies to literal or linguistic meanings. The logic of conversation applies to the rules that people use to infer what a speaker intends to convey, beginning with the literal meaning of an utterance and ending with an utterance meaning (also known as speaker meaning, intended meaning, or conveyed meaning). Grice's maxims of conversation follow from his cooperative principle: listeners assume that speakers will be truthful, relevant, clear, and informative. Normally, when a speaker intends the literal meaning of an utterance, these rules do not come into explicit play. However, these rules are systematically invoked whenever a speaker appears to violate a conversational maxim. Listeners assume that speakers will be cooperative. Therefore, whenever a maxim appears to be flouted, it will function as a conversational implicature—a signal that the speaker intends something other than the literal meaning of what has been said. If, for example, someone replies to an invitation to go to the movies by saying, "I have an exam tomorrow morning," then that reply will be taken as a rejection of the invitation. On the face of it, saying that one has an exam tomorrow is not a relevant response to an invitation. However, if the reply is assumed to be relevant, then it can be taken to imply that the person can't spare the time to go to the movies because she has to study for an impending exam.

Analogously, when someone says something that is literally false, then this too should function as a conversational implicature, that is, as a signal to search for a meaning that is not the literal meaning. When a proud father says, "My daughter is an angel," no one believes that she has wings. But a metaphor need not be literally false. The opposite assertion—that one's daughter is no angel—is literally true; she does not have wings. Yet this is not likely to be the speaker's intended meaning, nor is it likely to be a hearer's interpretation. In each of these two cases, hearers must go beyond the literal meaning to arrive at the speaker's intention—what the hearer is intended to understand. Searle put the issue clearly: "Where the utterance is defective if taken literally, look for an utterance meaning that differs from sentence meaning" (1979, p. 114).

This straightforward dictum leads directly to the standard three-stage model of nonliteral language comprehension proposed in linguistics (Lyons, 1977), as well as in philosophy (Grice, 1975; Searle, 1979) and in psychology (Clark & Lucy, 1975; Janus & Bever, 1985):

1. Derive the literal meaning of an utterance.
2. Test the derived literal meaning against the context of the utterance.
3. If the literal meaning makes sense, accept that meaning as the utterance meaning, that is, the speaker's intended meaning. If it does not make sense, then seek an alternative, nonliteral meaning that does make sense in the context.

The application of this general model to metaphor is straightforward. Metaphors are usually (although not always) false. They are therefore defective, in Searle's sense. When the hearer recognizes a metaphor as being false (or otherwise defective), she therefore implicitly transforms it from its false categorical form to its correspondingly true simile form. For example, the utterance *my lawyer is a shark* is literally false. By transforming it into the simile *My lawyer is like a shark*, the listener reframes it in such a way that it becomes true and therefore can be understood in the same way that any comparison assertion might be understood. Metaphors, on this view, are essentially implicit similes and so pose no further problems of interpretation.

There are four testable implications of this model. The first and most obvious is that literal meanings are unproblematic and context-free. The second is that literal meanings have unconditional priority. Because they have unconditional priority, they will always be derived first, before any nonliteral meanings are even attempted. Hence, they will always require less time and effort than nonliteral meanings. Third, because nonliteral meanings are sought if and only when literal meaning is "defective," there is an important difference between literal and nonliteral meanings. Literal meanings are derived automatically, but nonliteral meanings are derived only optionally. The term *automatic* here does not mean that literal understanding is not effortful or does not require complex computation. Instead, it means that a fluent speaker of a language has no voluntary control over whether or not an utterance such as "rocks are hard" will be understood. The language comprehender is data driven in the sense that given a linguistic input, it will process that input and generate a literal interpretation willy-nilly, whether or not it intends to (cf. Fodor, 1983). As Miller and Johnson-Laird put it, understanding "occurs automatically without conscious control by the listener: he (*sic*) cannot refuse to understand . . . loss of control over one's [language comprehension system] may correspond to knowing a language fluently" (1976, p. 166). According to the three-stage model I have outlined, such automaticity does not apply to nonliteral understanding. Nonliteral understanding must be triggered by the failure of a literal meaning to make sense in context. The fourth implication is that, because metaphors are (usually) literally false, they are implicitly transformed into true comparison statements and interpreted via a comparison process. I argue that each of these four claims is wrong. In this chapter, I try to show that literal language understanding is not context independent and unproblematic. In chapter 2, I examine the evidence showing that (a) nonliteral understanding is not in principle more effortful or more complex than literal understanding; (b) nonliteral understanding can be as data driven (i.e., automatic and nonoptional) as literal understanding; and (c) metaphors are not implicit comparisons and so are not understood via a comparison process.

Literal Meaning: Some Problems and Issues

What distinguishes literal from nonliteral meanings? There are two questions here. The first concerns how people judge whether a given interpretation is literal or not. The second concerns the ways in which literal meanings and nonliteral meanings are generated: do they rely on the same or on different sets of language-processing principles and mechanisms? Consider, first, the issue of recognizing whether or not a given meaning is literal. How do people recognize that an utterance is literal rather than nonliteral?

To address this question we need to distinguish between two kinds of operations: linguistic decoding and linguistic interpretation. Linguistic decoding involves only those operations that are theoretically defined as linguistic, namely, phonological, lexical, and syntactic operations. I stress "theoretically defined" because the literal meaning of an utterance cannot be identified apart from the linguistic theory that supplies the mechanism for analysis. Stern (2000) puts the issue succinctly: the "literal meaning of a simple expression is whatever our best linguistic theory tells us is its semantic interpretation . . . [The] literal meaning of a sentence is the rule-by-rule composition of the literal meanings of its constituents" (p. 23). On this view, literal meanings are an abstraction, restricted to what Lyons (1977) refers to as maximally decontextualized system-sentences.[9] Linguistic-literal meanings are thus the products of a particular (one hopes, the "best") theory of semantics and syntax, a theory that does not pretend to describe or explain what people actually do when talking and listening. Does this abstract theoretical construct have any functional utility in helping us understand how people decide whether an interpretation is literal or metaphorical?

Indirectly, yes. Just as theoretical linguistics defines the literal in terms of particular theories of the language system, so do speakers of a language define the literal in terms of their folk or intuitive theories of language.[10] Dictionaries presumably reflect common usage, and the *Oxford American Dictionary* provides a clue to our folk theory of language in the definition of the word *literal*: "in accordance with the primary meaning of a word or the actual words of a phrase, as contrasted with a metaphorical or exaggerated meaning." The entry also notes that "the word *literally* is sometimes used mistakenly (*sic*) in statements that are clearly not taken literally, as in *he was literally glued to the TV set every night*" (1980, p. 386). In our folk theory of language, words have primary meanings, and the literal meaning of a phrase or sentence is one that does not go beyond the primary meanings of the phrase or sentence constituents. Apart from formal linguistic theories, how are the primary, that is, literal, meanings of words identified?

One possibility would be to use the criterion of context dependence. A commonly held view is that literal language is real, true, unambiguous, and relatively context independent. Literal meaning is context independent in the sense that the meaning remains the same irrespective of the context of utterance. For example, we have the intuition that the sentence *dogs are animals* literally means the same thing no matter who utters it, when or where or to whom and under any circumstances. Nonliteral, in contrast, is felt to be open to alternative interpretations. A literal interpretation of the utterance *dogs are animals* would be something to the effect that dogs belong to the category of animals, as opposed to vegetables, minerals, or abstract ideas. A nonliteral interpretation could be something to the effect that dogs behave as they do because they are animals. The particular interpretation depends on the context of utterance. If the utterance is a reply to the complaint "Rex doesn't seem able to control his barking at night," then the assertion that dogs are animals might be an indirect way of saying that this behavior is not surprising because animals rarely can control themselves. In this interpretation, both the literal meaning and the additional indirect meaning constitute the conveyed meaning.

Under what circumstances can people make a purely literal interpretation—that dogs belong to the category of animals, period? It is difficult to imagine a context in which such a barebones interpretation would be made. Even if the assertion *dogs are animals* were intended to inform a listener of this fact, there would still be some interpretive work to do beyond the minimalist literal; for example, what alternatives to "animal" are intended? Are dogs animals as opposed to plants, or are dogs animals as opposed to rocks? As this example illustrates, even literal interpretations require contextual information beyond the linguistic meaning. The picture becomes even messier when we consider words whose meanings cannot be identified or specified without considering the context of use.

The logical connectives are one class of words whose meanings are context dependent. In formal logic, *if-then* has a specified, context-independent meaning. The assertion *if p then q* is true when the following conditions hold: *p and q, not p and q, not p and not q*. It is false when we have *p and not q*. If we substitute concrete events for *p* and *q*, then sometimes the logical meanings work, but often they do not. If instead of *p* and *q* we substitute *the sun shines tomorrow* and *we will go to the beach*, then we can consider the following alternative states of affairs:

1. p and *q*: The sun shines and we go to the beach.
2. *p* and not *q*: The sun shines and we do not go to the beach.
3. not *p* and *q*: The sun doesn't shine and we go to the beach.
4. not *p* and not *q*: The sun doesn't shine and we do not go to the beach.

Recall that *if p then q* is false only when we have *p and not q*, (ex. 2). Alternatives 1 and 4 seem to follow from the assertion *if the sun shines we go to the beach*, and so, both logically and pragmatically, they do not falsify this assertion. The third outcome poses a problem. Even it does not logically falsify the *if-then* assertion, it does seem to violate conversational expectations. To compound matters, the interpretation of *if-then* depends on particular contexts of use. There is a logical implication in the assertion *If you mow the lawn, then I'll pay you $5.00*. This implies that if you do not mow the lawn, then I will not pay you $5.00. No such logical implication appears, however, in the assertion *If you are a U.S. senator, then you are over thirty-five years old*. This does not imply that if you are not a U.S. senator, then you are not over thirty-five years old. In the latter case, the *if-then* expression states a prerequisite condition for being a senator; it does not state a logical relation.

Other connectives display the same variability in natural language use. In logic, *p AND q* is true whenever *p* is true and *q* is true. In natural language, the word *AND* can be used to express a variety of relations:

1. Do that one more time and I'll smack you (an *if-then* relation).
2. Mark is a genius and there are twenty inches in a foot (sarcastic denial of Mark's genius status, paraphrasable in the *if-then* form).
3. Mark is a lawyer and Mark is a lawyer (logically true, conversationally inane).

In natural language, then, the primary meanings of connectives are not context independent, yet people treat them as literal nonetheless.

Other classes of words whose meanings are explicitly context dependent include quantifiers (some, a few, many), deictic terms (here, there, in this place), adjectives (good, tall, expensive), and pronouns (he, she, them). One cannot know what these terms refer to outside their contexts of use. *A few people in the kitchen* would be taken to mean four or five people; *a few people in the football stadium* might mean several thousand (Horman, 1983). *Christmas is here* refers to a time. *The newspaper is here* could mean that it has been delivered, is available at the newsstand, or is in the kitten's litter box. If the first of these, then we already have it to read; if the second, it is potentially available if we go out and buy it; if the third, it is not something to be read at all. And what are we to make of words such as *good* when meanings can vary so enormously (Bierwisch, 1967):

1. He got a good whipping for being late; good = painful?
2. Harry Truman was a good president; good = honest, effective?
3. Hannibal Lecter was more than just a good villain; good = ruthless, vicious, terrifying?

Are these examples limited to these particular classes of words, or do we also see context dependence in ordinary nouns and verbs?

The word *line* couldn't be more ordinary. It is a word that is used very frequently, and as a noun its primary or core meaning involves the notion of extension (Caramazza & Grober, 1976). But, even with this common semantic feature of extension, different contexts of use induce different interpretations:

1. Sam owned the local bus line.
2. She said it was a line from Keats.
3. The rich man was able to line his pocket with money.
4. Sergeant Jones would bring him into line.
5. The judge had to draw a line between right and wrong.
6. I pulled on the line with all my strength.
7. The shortest distance between two points is a straight line.

Analogously, the word *open* has different, albeit related, interpretations in different contexts.

1. He opened the box of cookies.
2. She opened the conversation by commenting on the weather.
3. The surgeon opened the patient's chest.
4. He opened his eyes.
5. She kept an open mind.
6. He opened Pandora's box.
7. He opened her eyes to her husband's infidelities.

There seems to be a common core of meaning to all of these uses of *open*, even when it is used metaphorically, as in 6 and 7 (and perhaps 5?). What distinguishes the literal uses from the metaphorical ones? It cannot be in the way that context is used to arrive at an interpretation. It also cannot be in any differences in conventionality. The expression *open mind* may not even qualify as metaphorical, while *opening Pandora's box* and *opening someone's eyes to something* border on cliché.

Perhaps the most useful position is that the concept of *literal* cannot be explicitly defined except in formal linguistic-theory terms. Within our folk theory of language, we make a sharp distinction between the literal and the nonliteral. However, when we make judgments about specific examples, the distinctions become graded, rather than discrete. People can make reliable judgments about degrees of metaphoricity, for example, suggesting that there is a continuum from the literal to the nonliteral (Ortony, 1979).

In this respect, the concept of literal (or the concept of metaphorical, for that matter) behaves as do other natural-kind concepts. For natural-kind concepts, such as *fruits*, there are clear, prototypical examples, such as apples, pears and bananas. There are also not so clear, nonprototypical examples, such as pumpkin, tomato, and olive (McCloskey & Glucksberg, 1978). People are unanimous when asked if an apple is a fruit but disagree about tomatoes, even though both apples and tomatoes are, technically (literally?) fruits: they are the fruiting bodies of their plants and have seeds.

Our best definition of the concept of literal meaning, then, is analogous to our best definitions of natural-kind concepts. On the one hand, experts have explicit theories for assigning candidate exemplars to their appropriate categories. Linguists have a theory of the lexicon, of syntax, and semantics. Analogously, botanists have a theory of plant life and biological taxonomies. Within such theories, clear categorical distinctions can often be made. On the other hand, lay persons have implicit folk theories from which to make categorical judgments, and, in both the language case and the botanical case, graded judgments seem to be the rule, even when elements of the technical theory are, in principle, available. Thus, even though we may know the technical definition of *fruit* as "the edible product of a tree, shrub or other plant, consisting of the seed and its envelope" (*Oxford English Dictionary*, 1996), we are reluctant to say that a tomato, a pumpkin, or an olive is a fruit. Our folk theory of plants and foods leads us to assign these exemplars to different categories on a probabilistic, rather than a determinate, basis. Similarly, even though we may know that the expression *glued to the TV set* does not use the primary meaning of the verb *to glue*, we still feel that this is a perfectly straightforward, literal-like usage. Perhaps it is this double awareness—of the technically nonliteral and of the simultaneously perfectly straightforward usage—that prompts people to produce what is technically a contradiction: describing metaphorical expressions as *literal*, as in *he was literally glued to the TV set*. Technically, *glued to the TV set* is a metaphor, but intuitively it is literal, just as technically a tomato is a fruit but intuitively it's a vegetable.

These examples imply that metaphor appreciation and metaphor understanding may be independent of one another (see Gerrig & Healy, 1983). Much like Moliere's character M. Jourdain in *Le Bourgeois Gentilhomme*, who was amazed and delighted to learn that he spoke in prose (Moliere, 1675), people may use and understand metaphorical expressions without being aware that the expressions are metaphorical at all. This should certainly be the case if metaphor and literal understanding depend on the same linguistic, cognitive, and pragmatic principles. However, our intuitive folk theory of language views literal meaning as primary meaning. Is this merely an intuition about the appreciation of a difference between literal and metaphorical expressions, or does it also reflect differences in modes and ease of processing? We consider the evidence on this issue in chapter 2.

Beyond the Literal

Midway between the unintelligible and the commonplace, it is a metaphor
most which produces knowledge

Aristotle, 1410 B.C.

Are literal meanings functionally primary? Recall the distinction between
linguistic decoding and linguistic interpretation. Decoding refers exclusively to purely linguistic operations: phonological, lexical, and syntactic.
Decoding an utterance results in a literal meaning. Does a literal interpretation require people to go beyond a decoded literal meaning? An example
from a recent *New York Times* headline makes clear the need to go beyond
bare-bones literal meanings: *Price Soars for Eggs, Setting Off a Debate on
a Clinic's Ethics.* The linguistic literal meaning is not at issue here. Each
of the words and phrases in the heading is intended in its primary, literal
sense. *Eggs* refers to eggs (but what kind?); *prices* refers to the cost of
something (but at what level?); *clinic* refers to the medical sense of clinic
(but what kind?); *ethics* refers to what people ordinarily think of as ethics
and morals. It is not until one reads further that one learns that the eggs
that are referred to are not the sort that one scrambles for breakfast but
instead are human ova that, if fertilized and implanted in a womb, develop
into human babies. The clinic is a fertility clinic, and the issue is whether
or not young women should sell or "donate" their ova for artificial insem-
ination and implantation in donee mothers. The egg providers can be
viewed as "donors" if they receive some small remuneration for their time
and trouble; they would be viewed as sellers if they were to receive a lot
of money. The ethical issue is whether or not human ova should be sold
for profit. The deceptively simple, literally intended headline turns out to
require a wealth of biological, medical, social, cultural, theological, economic, and sociological knowledge to be understood as intended. Granted,

this is a particularly complex case, but even the simplest utterances require more than linguistic decoding.

Consider again the standard pragmatic three-stage model of metaphor processing. The first step is to derive a literal meaning. That meaning is then tested against the context; if it is uninterpretable, then alternative non literal meanings are sought. The price-of-eggs example points up a thorny problem. The context that enabled us to interpret the price-of-eggs head-line led us to seek not an alternative nonliteral meaning, but rather a particular *literal* interpretation. Pure linguistic decoding did not suffice for a contextually appropriate literal interpretation. [1] Examples such as this have led theorists such as Searle (1993) to argue that literal decoding must always be augmented by contextual information before that decoded mean-ing can be accepted or used for interpretation, even for a literal interpre-tation.

Some scholars go beyond even this claim, arguing that literal decoding per se requires the use of information beyond the purely linguistic. Clark (1996) cites this example from British English: the word *garage* can be used literally in either of two senses, to refer to a parking structure or to a repair facility. Thus, if someone says, "I'm taking the car to the garage," it is not clear whether the car will be parked or repaired. How, then, do people decide which meaning is intended? The answer, of course, is con-text. Imagine these two different scenarios. George telephones home and says to his wife:

1. I just got to the hardware store and discovered I had a flat tire.
2. I just got to the hardware store, but there's no place to park.

George's wife replies, "There's a garage around the corner on Pine Street." Her reference to "a garage" in either circumstance is unambiguous. George will understand it to refer in the first instance to a repair facility, in the second to a parking facility. Is this understanding immediate, or does George have to consider both meanings and then opt for the appropriate one only after considering the context of his own utterance? There is a voluminous literature on how such lexical ambiguities are resolved. The preponderance of the evidence suggests that the contextually appropriate meaning is selectively accessed whenever the context makes absolutely clear which meaning of an ambiguous word is intended (Simpson & Kreuger, 1991). Even the process of word recognition is context sensitive. Contex-tual information is used even before a word has been fully heard, beginning with the perception of a word's initial phonemes (Marslen-Wilson & Welsh, 1978; Tannenhaus, Spivey-Knowlton, Eberhard, & Sedivy, 1995, 1996).

The implications for metaphor processing are unequivocal. When one encounters a metaphorical expression, there is no principled reason for a literal interpretation to take precedence over a metaphorical one, given that even initial word recognition and literal decoding are context sensitive. Are metaphorical interpretations as available as literal ones from the very be-

ginning of processing? If they are, then it should take no more time to understand a metaphor than to understand a comparable literal expression. In one of the first studies to examine this issue, Ortony and his colleagues (Ortony, Schallert, Reynolds, & Antos, 1978) compared the time people took to understand sentential metaphors—sentences that, depending on the context of utterance, can be interpreted either literally or metaphorically. For example, the sentence *regardless of the danger, the troops marched on* could appear at the end of either of these two passages:
    Literal context:

Approaching the enemy infantry, the men worried about touching off land mines. They were anxious that their presence would be detected prematurely. Their fears were compounded by the knowledge that they might be isolated from their reinforcements. The outlook was grim.
    Regardless of the danger, the troops marched on.

Metaphorical context:

The children continued to annoy their babysitter. She told the little boys she would not tolerate any more bad behavior. Climbing all over the furniture was not allowed. She threatened to spank them if they continued to stomp, run, and scream around the room. The children knew that her spankings hurt.
    Regardless of the danger, the troops marched on.

In the context of the narrative about infantry in combat, the sentence should be interpreted literally. *The danger* is taken to refer to the possibility of being wounded or killed by land mines, the *troops* refers to soldiers in the field, and *marched on* refers to soldiers pressing forward on foot. In the context of a story about rebellious children being threatened by an angry babysitter, the sentence is interpreted metaphorically. *The troops* in this case refers to the children, the *danger* is now taken to refer to the possibility of being spanked by the babysitter, and *marched on* refers to boisterous behavior. Does this metaphorical interpretation take more time to arrive at than the literal? Ortony et al. (1978) measured the time people took to read the last sentence of each context passage. When the context passage consisted of only the first sentence, followed immediately by the test sentence, people did take more time to understand the metaphorical test sentences (4.4 sec) than the literal ones (3.6 sec). In contrast, when the full contexts were used, the advantage of the literal disappeared. Both sentence types took less time than in the abbreviated contexts, and the metaphorical took no longer than the literal (1.9 sec and 2.1 sec, respectively; times approximated from figure 1 in Ortony et al., 1978).
    These findings were replicated by Inhoff, Lima, and Carroll (1984), who used eye-tracking measures to compare the time people took to focus on appropriate words as they read either literal or metaphorical test sentences. As in the Ortony et al. study, both short and long story contexts were used. The subjects read metaphors just as quickly as literal sentences, regardless of context length, reinforcing the conclusion that metaphors in

context are no more difficult to understand than literally intended sentences. However, some object to this kind of study arguing that the times used to assess the relative difficulty of comprehending the sentences tend to be quite long, on the order of 2.5 to 5 seconds. In terms of normal language comprehension, 5 seconds to read an eight-word sentence is a long time, considering that normal reading speeds run from 250 to 350 words per minute. At a rate of 300 words per minute, an eight-word sentence should be read in only 1.6 seconds. It may be that any differences in reading time between literal and metaphorical sentences are masked by other processes, such as the time needed to integrate a sentence interpretation with the preceding context, the time taken to decide that a test sentence has been understood, and the time taken to make the appropriate response. Eye-movement data avoid some of these potentially confounding component processes but pose an equally thorny problem. With only eye-movement measures, we cannot be sure that metaphorical test sentences are actually interpreted metaphorically. All we can be sure of is that the time to fixate certain words is the same for metaphorically intended and literally intended test sentences. We do not know if the conveyed interpretations were congruent with the intended interpretations.

A more recent study by Blasko and Connine (1993) used a cross-modal priming paradigm to address more directly the issue of processing time. Their experiment took advantage of the phenomenon of semantic priming. One measure of the relative accessibility of a particular word's meaning is the time people take to read that word and to decide whether or not it is a word in the English language. When a target word appears immediately after a semantically related word, then lexical decisions are made more quickly than when it appears after an unrelated word. For example, people need less time to decide that *nurse* is a word when it is preceded by the word *doctor* than when it is preceded by the word *radio*. This technique has been used to study which meanings of ambiguous words are activated in different contexts (Onifer & Swinney, 1981; Simpson & Kreuger, 1991). Blasko and Connine adapted the technique to assess whether metaphorical meanings can be activated as quickly as literal meanings. The people who participated in the experiments listened to metaphorical phrases in neutral contexts, such as: "Jerry first knew that *loneliness was a desert** when he was very young****." The experimental task was to listen to each sentence; while the participants were listening, a letter string target would appear on a computer screen, either immediately after the metaphor (where * appears in the example) or 300 milliseconds (msec) later (where ** appears in the example). When the visual target appeared, the participants had to decide, as quickly and as accurately as they could, whether or not it was an English word. On half of all the trials the target was a word, and on half the trials it was a nonword. There were three types of word targets, defined in terms of their relation to the metaphorical phrase: metaphorical, literal, and control. For the *loneliness is a desert* metaphor, the metaphorical, literal, and control targets were, respectively, *Isolate, Sand,* and *Mustache*.

Faster lexical decisions to metaphorical or literal targets relative to control targets would indicate activation of metaphorical or literal meanings, respectively.

Literal targets were faster than controls both immediately and after the 300–msec delay, indicating that literal meanings were always activated. This finding is consistent with Giora's graded salience hypothesis, which states that all salient meanings of a word are activated regardless of context (Giora, 1977, in press). Metaphorical targets were also activated faster than controls at both delays, but only when the metaphors were considered to be apt, that is, when they were rated as good metaphors by an independent group of experimental participants. The metaphorical meanings of these apt metaphors were thus understood as quickly as the literal meanings, even when the metaphors were relatively unfamiliar.

These results are consistent with those of other studies of metaphor comprehension that have found no differences in the time taken to understand metaphorically and literally intended expressions (Harris, 1976; Onishi & Murphy, 1993; Pynte, Besson, Robichon & Poli, 1996). However, Blasko and Connine's results seem to be inconsistent with those of studies of ambiguity resolution in context. When people interpret ambiguous words, either context-inappropriate meanings are either not activated at all or, if they are, then their activation does not continue beyond 250 msec (Onifer & Swinney, 1981). In Blasko and Connine's study, the literal meanings remained active for at least 300 msec. One reason for this difference might be the nature of the literally related targets that were used. In many of the items, the "literally related" target word was also related to the metaphor and could even be substituted for the metaphor vehicle and still make metaphorical sense. One example of an unfamiliar but apt metaphor that poses this potential problem is *his anger is a blizzard*. The metaphor and literal target words for this item were *blinding* and *snowing*, respectively. It is not surprising that *snowing* remains highly accessible 300 msec after the word *blizzard*. The literal and metaphorical meanings are highly related.

This study, then, tells us that metaphorical meanings can be accessed as quickly as literal ones, but it tells us nothing about the fate of contextually inappropriate literal meanings. In order to assess the fate of contextually inappropriate literal meanings, Newsome replicated the Blasko and Connine study but added a condition in which the literally related target words were completely unrelated to the metaphor (e.g., instead of the word *snowing* for the metaphorical blizzard, Newsome used the target word *snowflake*). The word *snowflake* is certainly related to the word *blizzard*, but it connotes gentleness and softness rather than the anger-related sense of *blizzard*. Under these conditions, literal meanings that are not related to the metaphor were not activated, either immediately or 500 msec later (Newsome, 1999). These results stongly suggest that contextually inappropriate literal meanings are not always activated in metaphor contexts and certainly are not retained as part of what's understood when people interpret metaphors. We address this issue in more detail in chapter 4. We turn now to a second implication of the traditional view that literal meaning has unconditional priority. As we noted earlier, fluent speakers of a language do not have the option of refusing to understand; the language processor is data driven. Any linguistic input will be processed, phonologically, lexically, and syntactically (Miller & Johnson-Laird, 1976; Fodor, 1983). This guarantees that literal meanings are nonoptional; they will always be generated, regardless of context. Are metaphorical meanings also automatically generated, or is metaphor comprehension optional, dependent on context?

On the Optionality of Figurative Meaning:
Can People Ignore Metaphors?

In the studies that examined the relative speed of literal and metaphorical comprehension, people were either explicitly or implicitly instructed to attend to and understand metaphorical expressions. Will people generate metaphorical interpretations even when there is no obvious reason to do so? Standard pragmatic theory, following Grice and Searle, is clear on this issue. Nonliteral meanings, including metaphorical meanings, are generated only when an utterance is "defective": "Where the utterance is defective if taken literally, look for an utterance meaning that differs from sentence [i.e., literal] meaning" (Searle, 1979, p. 114). Utterances are defective when they seem to violate rules of conversation (Grice, 1975) or otherwise make no sense in context (Clark & Lucy, 1975).

An alternative view draws a distinction between linguistic decoding and literal interpretation. Before any kind of interpretation can be generated, utterances must be decoded (phonologically for spoken language, orthographically for written text), lexically and syntactically, at least to some minimal extent.[2] Once decoded, utterances must then be interpreted: literally, figuratively, or both. What determines whether metaphorical interpretations are generated? The strongest claim for the automaticity of metaphor comprehension is that metaphorical meanings are apprehended whenever they are available. This implies that people are not able to ignore metaphors, even when literal meanings make perfect sense in context. We assessed this hypothesis in a series of experiments in which people would perform optimally if they attended exclusively to literal meanings while ignoring metaphorical ones (Glucksberg, Gildea, & Bookin, 1982; Keysar, 1989). The experiments were modeled after Stroop's (1935) classic demonstration that people cannot ignore literal meanings. Stroop presented words printed in various colors and asked people to name the color of the ink, *not* to read the words themselves. When color words such as *red* were printed in any color other than red (e.g., in green), people had difficulty saying "green," indicating that they were experiencing response competition from the involuntary reading of the word itself *red*. This color-word interference effect was taken to mean that people could not inhibit their reading of words that were attended to, even when such inhibition would have improved their task performance.

We applied this logic to literally false but metaphorically true sentences such as "some roads are snakes" and "some offices are icebergs." Our experimental participants were shown sentences one at a time on a screen and instructed to judge whether each sentence was literally true or false. We used four different kinds of sentences: literally true (e.g., *some birds are robins*); literally false (e.g., *some birds are apples*); metaphors (e.g., *some jobs are jails, some flutes are birds*); and scrambled metaphors (e.g., *some jobs are birds, some flutes are jails*). The metaphors were literally false category-membership assertions, but they were readily interpretable if taken non-literally. The scrambled metaphors were also literally false, but not readily interpretable.

If people could ignore the metaphorical meanings, then the participants should take no longer to reject the metaphors than the scrambled metaphors. If, on the other hand, people automatically register any metaphorical meanings that are available, then the participants should take longer to judge as false the metaphor sentences than to reach the same conclusion about their scrambled counterparts; this because of the response competition between the "true" nonliteral meanings and the "false" literal meanings of the metaphor sentences. Our results were clear-cut. People had difficulty in rejecting the metaphors as literally false. The mean response time to reject metaphor sentences (1239 msec) was reliably longer than the time to reject either literally false sentences (1185 msec) or scrambled metaphors (1162 msec). Furthermore, this effect was not the result of mere associations between metaphor topics and vehicles but of an appreciation of metaphorical meaning itself. If an association between topic and vehicle is sufficient for the interference effect, then should make no difference which quantifier, *all* or *some*, is used, but it does. Metaphors that are judged to be good in the *some* form but poor in the *all* form behave differentially. For example, people tend to agree that *some surgeons are butchers* but don't agree that *all surgeons are butchers*. Not surprisingly, *some surgeons are butchers* produces the metaphor interference effect, but *all surgeons are butchers* does not. We interpreted this metaphor interference effect in the same way that Stroop interpreted his color-word interference effect: people could not inhibit their understanding of metaphorical meanings, even when literal meanings were acceptable in the context of our experiment.

When metaphorical meanings are not immediately available, then a minimal context can make them so (Gildea & Glucksberg, 1983). Consider the novel but rather clumsy metaphor *all marriages are iceboxes*. Normally, this metaphor does not produce a metaphor interference effect in our Stroop-like experimental paradigm. This indicates that people do not automatically get one of its several potential metaphorical meanings. One interpretation of this metaphor is that marriages are cold and unemotional. How can this interpretation be primed, that is, made salient? We reasoned that any context that would activate a property of the metaphor vehicle that would be informative about the topic would be sufficient to trigger immediate comprehension. A potentially informative property of the metaphor vehicle *iceboxes* might be *cold*. A relevant dimension along which to characterize marriages might be emotional warmth or, more generally, emotional temperature.

We modified our original sentence verification paradigm so that we could assess the relative effectiveness of various types of contexts for immediate comprehension of novel (and rather clumsy) metaphors. Again, people were asked to respond to the literal truth value of simple sentences, and again our index for whether or not a metaphor was understood rapidly and automatically was whether or not a literal-false decision was slowed down. The metaphors that we used do not normally produce an interference effect. Would they produce such an effect if we made the concept of coldness salient, either in its figurative sense of emotional quality or in its literal sense of physical temperature? We wanted to provide such contexts unobtrusively, and so we simply preceded the metaphor target sentences with one of three kinds of sentences:

1. an unrelated sentence, such as *some mountains are big*; or
2. a metaphor-relevant figurative sentence (e.g., *some people are cold*); or
3. a metaphor-relevant literal sentence (e.g., *some winters are cold*).

If metaphor comprehension were somehow different in kind from literal comprehension, then we might expect that the figurative context sentences would be more effective primes than the literal context sentences. Somewhat surprisingly, the two kinds of relevant primes were equally effective. When the metaphors followed unrelated sentences, we observed no metaphor interference. When the metaphors followed either literally or figuratively related sentences, we found that people were slower to judge them literally false, suggesting that the metaphors had been rapidly and automatically understood.[3]

Is it necessary to activate a specific concept such as *cold* to make these metaphors immediately comprehensible, or is it sufficient to merely remind people of the relevant dimension of temperature? To assess this possibility, we conducted a second experiment in which we used general literal context sentences instead of specific ones. For example, for the marriages-iceboxes metaphor we used *some summers are warm* instead of *some winters are cold*. Not only is this context sentence literal, but the relevant word, *warm*, is the antonym of the ground of the metaphor, *cold*. To our surprise, even this minimal context rendered the marriages-iceboxes metaphor immediately comprehensible. What information did such contexts provide? The general literal contexts provided a relevant dimension upon which the metaphor topic, could be characterized, in this case, temperature broadly conceived. Apparently, this was enough to allow them to disambiguate the metaphors, making their interpretation nonproblematic. They were now comprehended rapidly enough to produce the metaphor interference effect (i.e., people were slow to decide that these sentences were literally false) (see also Shinjo & Myers, 1987).

Perhaps the most convincing evidence that metaphorical interpretations are generated in parallel with literal ones was provided by McElree and his colleagues (McElree & Griffith, 1995; McElree & Nordlie, 1999). As in our studies of the metaphor interference effect, McElree and Nordlie asked people to judge the literal truth value of sentences that were literally false but metaphorically true. In addition, they used a meaningfulness judgment task to see if, in an analogous fashion, literal falsehood interfered with people's ability to judge that "true" metaphors were meaningful. Instead of using simple reaction time measures, however, McElree and Nordlie used a speed-accuracy trade-off procedure to examine the time course of sentence interpretation. In general, there is an inverse relation between speed and accuracy in any given task. Depending on the criterion adopted, people can either emphasize speed while sacrificing accuracy or sacrifice speed in favor of greater accuracy. This inverse relation obtains whenever performance depends on an accumulation of information over time. Judging whether or not a sentence is literally true is just such a task. Lexical access, syntactic analysis, and semantic interpretation all take time. If a person responds "true" or "false" before these processes are completed, she will not have accumulated enough information to ensure that her response is accurate. The less time she takes, the less information she will have accumulated, making errors more likely. Judging whether or not a sentence is meaningful also involves incremental accumulation of information; accuracy varies with response time in this task as well. The faster the response, the lower the accuracy, and vice versa.

The trade-off between speed and accuracy can be influenced by instructions (e.g., when people are told that speed is more important than accuracy or vice versa). The trade-off can also be controlled experimentally by forcing people to respond before they can fully process the relevant material. For example, a person might be asked to judge whether a sentence is literally true or false but be forced to respond within 250 msec. At that speed, accuracy will be at chance level because the person has not had enough time to accumulate any relevant information. If the person can wait, say, half a second before responding, he might have gathered enough information for his performance to be above chance level, but there will still be a high likelihood of errors. If the person is given, say, 3 seconds before he must respond, then his accuracy could well be at asymptote (i.e., as high as it can get, given the difficulty of the particular task).

The time people have available to accumulate information before responding can be controlled by a response deadline procedure. For a sentence judgment task, the experimenter can flash a sentence on a computer screen, one word at a time, at a rate of 200 msec per word. After the last word appears on the screen, the experimenter sounds a short tone as a response cue, and the participant must respond whenever that cue occurs. The response cue can sound as soon as 10 msec or as long as 3 seconds after the last word of the sentence. Obviously, after only 10 msec the participant does not have enough information to make any judgment at all, and so we would expect performance to be no better than at chance level. After 3 seconds, she should have enough information to make very accurate decisions, and so we would expect performance to be as good as it can get (i.e., at asymptote). Figure 2.1 provides an example of a typical speed-accuracy trade-off function. At very short time lags, performance is no better than chance, represented as zero accuracy in figure 2.1. With longer lags, more information accumulates. When enough information accumulates, performance begins to rise above chance level, as represented by the intercept in figure 2.1. Performance improves incrementally until it reaches asymptote, the maximum accuracy for the particular task. The rate at which information accumulates is represented by the time for the function to reach asymptote. For tasks that involve relatively easy decisions, asymptote is very high; for more difficult decisions, asymptote is lower.

How might the speed-accuracy trade-off functions for literal and metaphoric processes differ? One obvious difference would be in asymptotic level: either literal or metaphorical decisions might be easier, depending on the particular materials used. Thus, differences in asymptotic performance level would tell us nothing about the time-courses of literal and metaphoric processing. The functions might also differ in intercept (the time lag when performance gets better than chance), and they might also differ in rate of improvement. Figures 2.2a and 2.2b illustrate two possible sets of speed-accuracy trade-off functions, each for two sources of infor-

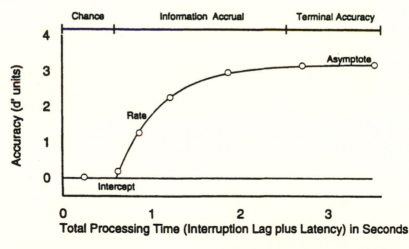

Figure 2.1. A typical speed-accuracy trade-off (SAT) function for reaction time data obtained with the response deadline procedure (after McElree & Griffith, 1995).

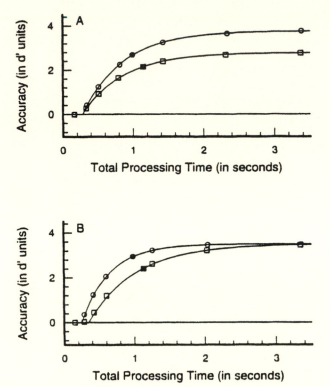

Figure 2.2. Hypothetical speed-accuracy trade-off (SAT) functions illustrating two conditions that differ by (A) SAT asymptote only or (B) SAT intercept and rate. Function A reflects two processes that operate in parallel with equal time-courses. Function B reflects two processes that operate independently and sequentially, with different time-courses (after McElree and Nordlie, 1999).

mation. If the two functions differ only in asymptotic level, then this means that the two independent information sources (for example, a literal and a metaphorical information source) have equal time-courses. Information about literal meaning and about metaphorical meaning is available at the same time for performance to be better than chance, as indicated by both functions having the same intercept (Figure 2.2a). Information about literal and metaphorical meanings accumulates at the same rate, even though they may reach different asymptotes, as indicated by the equal times to reach asymptote. The difference between the two functions remains constant after a brief rise from zero, indicating that the two functions differ only in asymptotic level.

The functions shown in figure 2.2b would be produced by a two-stage, sequential processing system. An example of such a system is one in which literal meaning is obtained first and is then used to generate metaphorical meaning. In contrast to the functions shown for the parallel processes with equal time-courses, the rate of information accumulation differs for the two sources, literal and metaphorical. Even if we assume equivalent asymptotes, accuracy for literal meaning is higher than for the metaphorical until asymptotes are reached. This is reflected in the difference between the two functions. This difference increases rapidly from the intercept time (when performance first exceeds chance), then decreases gradually to zero as both processes reach asymptote (McElree & Griffith, 1995, 1998).

McElree and Nordlie (1999) applied this logic using the response deadline procedure in the metaphor-interference paradigm, where judgments about literally false sentences are slowed when the sentences are metaphorically true. They obtained speed-accuracy trade-off functions that were consistent with a system that used parallel information sources with equal time-courses, similar to those in figure 2.2a. Similar functions were obtained when people made meaningfulness judgments instead of literal-truth judgments. The conclusions are straightforward: people generate literal and metaphorical interpretations in parallel, and the time-courses for the two parallel processes are the same. Neither literal nor metaphorical interpretations take priority, at least for the kinds of metaphors used in these experiments.[4]

In the studies that we have just reviewed, the critical sentences were always literally false but metaphorically true. Would metaphors that are false in a given context also be understood automatically? Perhaps there is a weaker form of literal priority such that literal meanings are generated regardless of truth value, but metaphors are understood only if they make sense in context (Dascal, 1987). Would there be any evidence for automaticity of metaphorical meanings when sentences are literally true but metaphorically false in context? A series of elegant experiments by Keysar (1989) assessed this idea. People were given brief story-vignettes to read, one at a time. Each story was followed by a target sentence that, in the context of the story, could be literally true or false as well as metaphorically true or false. The experimental task was to decide whether the target sentence was *literally* true or false. An example of a story with a literally true but metaphorically false target sentence is:

> Bob Jones is an expert at such stunts as sawing a woman in half and pulling rabbits out of hats. He earns his living traveling around the world with an expensive entourage of equipment and assistants. Although Bob tries to budget carefully, it seems to him that money just disappears into thin air. With such huge audiences, why doesn't he ever break even?
> Target Sentence: *Bob Jones is a magician.*

In this context, Bob is literally a magician but isn't able to make his financial worries disappear and so, metaphorically speaking, he is certainly not a magician. Because of this mismatch between literal and metaphorical truth, people take longer to decide that the target sentence is literally true. When the story describes Bob both literally and figuratively as a magician, people are very quick to agree that he is literally a magician. We can thus find a metaphor interference effect even when a sentence is literally true but metaphorically false. Metaphorical interpretations seem to be generated whenever they are available, irrespective of whether they make sense in context. In this respect, they are fully comparable to literal interpretations.

People also spontaneously apprehend metaphorical meanings even when they are only implicitly available, as in noun-noun compounds. Many noun-noun compounds can be interpreted either metaphorically or literally (Wisniewski, 1997). For example, if the compound *shark lawyer* is interpreted as a lawyer who is predatory and aggressive, then the noun *shark* is used to refer to a metaphorical rather than a literal shark. If the same compound is interpreted as a lawyer who represents sharks (as in, perhaps, a legal matter involving protection of sharks as an endangered species), then *shark* refers to the literal shark, that is, the marine creature. Similarly, compounds such *movie life* can be interpreted either metaphorically (e.g., as in *his life is a movie)* or literally, (referring to the life of people who work in movies). We gave noun-noun combinations to college students and asked for their interpretations. People overwhelmingly chose to interpret combinations as metaphorical rather than literal whenever metaphorical interpretations were available (Goldvarg & Glucksberg, 1998). Clearly, people are finely attuned to finding metaphorical meanings, even when they are not the only alternative and even when they are presented implicitly in noun-noun compound form rather than in explicit metaphor or simile form.

We can conclude that genus-for-genus metaphors—those in the form *X is a Y*—are understood as rapidly as comparable literal expressions. Furthermore, metaphorical and literal interpretations are generated in parallel, and the time-courses of the two processes are the same in all relevant respects. And, like literally intended expressions, comprehension is non-optional. We can no more shut off our metaphor-understanding machinery than our literal-understanding machinery. We now turn to an examination of that machinery: how do people understand metaphors such as *the mind is a machine?*

Beyond Similarity

It would be more illuminating . . . to say that the metaphor creates the similarity than to say that it formulates some similarity antecedently existing.

Max Black, 1962

We have examined two of the three psychological implications of the standard pragmatic theory of metaphor comprehension: that metaphor understanding is more difficult than literal and that literal understanding has unconditional priority. Both of these implications turned out to be false. The third implication is that metaphors, once recognized as such, are treated as implicit similes. According to the theory, when one encounters a literally false sentence such as *cigarettes are time bombs*, it is implicitly transformed into the literally true sentence *cigarettes are like time bombs*. It can then be treated as any ordinary comparison statement. As Ortony (1979) put it, a metaphor is an indirect comparison, whereas a simile is a direct comparison, albeit a metaphorical one. This view is often attributed to Aristotle, even though Aristotle's position was more akin to Black's and, as we shall make clear, our own (see also Kittay, 1987). For Aristotle, as for Black, metaphors are not similes. Rather, similes are metaphors: "The simile also is a metaphor; the difference is but slight" (in *Rhetoric*, cited by Stern, 2000).

Which comes first, the metaphorical egg or the chicken of similitude? Our first task is to evaluate the adequacy of similarity as a basis for understanding metaphor: to what extent can our best models of literal similarity account for metaphorical similarity? If similarity fails as an explanatory mechanism, then our second task will be to develop an alternative that (a) accounts for how people interpret metaphors and (b) also explicates the relation between metaphor and simile.

Metaphor as Implicit Simile: The Contrast Model

How do people interpret comparison statements of the form *a is like b*? Amos Tversky, in his classic paper "Features of Similarity" (1977), proposed that such statements are assessed by comparing the features of *a* with the features of *b*. Note that Tversky used the term *assessed* and not *comprehended*. The reason for this is that his model of similarity addresses the issue of how people judge the degree of similarity between two concepts, not how comparison statements are initially understood. As we shall see, Tversky's comparison model presupposes comprehension rather than accounts for it.

The first and most obvious characteristic of people's interpretations of comparisons is that not all of the features of the two terms *a* and *b* are included. Instead, only relevant subsets of the features of *a* and of the features of *b* is selected for consideration. For example, if someone says that *Harvard is like Yale*, people do not normally take this to mean that both Harvard and Yale have brick buildings, that they have students, a faculty, deans, an admissions office, a library, a computer center, dormitories, and heating and cooling systems. Not even the defining features of universities would be considered under normal circumstances. We presuppose that Harvard and Yale are alike in their essentials, whatever the essentials of a university might be, and so these features are considered irrelevant. Relevant features might include size of endowment, characteristics of student bodies, tuition, prestige of their law schools, and relative success in attracting research funds.

Because the number of features that can be attributed in common to any two objects is unlimited (Weinrich, 1966), any theory of feature matching must either provide some mechanism for extracting subsets of features that are relevant in a given context or simply postulate prior feature selection and proceed from there. Tversky is clear on this point: "the representation of an object as a collection of features is viewed as a *product of a prior process* of extraction and compilation" (1977, pp. 329–330, emphasis added). The prior process of extraction and compilation, however, can be nothing other than the interpretation of the comparison assertion itself. To understand a comparison is to identify the respects in which the two terms are alike, namely the grounds for the comparison. Thus, the contrast model is not intended as a model of how comparisons are understood. Instead, it is a model of how people judge the degree to which two objects are similar, given that the bases for the similarity—that is, the relevant features that both are and are not in common—have already been identified.

The contrast model was explicitly developed for literal similarity. How well does it account for judgments of metaphorical similarity? According to the model, relevant features are initially selected and compiled. Two kinds of relevant features are included: those that are in common to the two objects and those that are not. For example, if one were to compare hotels and motels, relevant features in common would include guest rooms with beds; relevant features not in common would include parking close to one's room for motels but typically not for hotels. As Gentner and her colleagues have pointed out, there can be no similarity without relevant differences (Gentner & Markman, 1994). Once the relevant features have been selected, the perceived similarity s between two objects a and b is a weighted function of features that are common to a and b, and of features that are distinctive, that is, not common to a and b:

$$s(a,b) = \theta f(A \cap B) - \alpha f(A - B) - \beta f(B - A)$$

where θ is the weight assigned to features that are common to the objects, α is the weight assigned to features of a that are not included in b, and β is the weight assigned to features of b that are not included in a. Differential weighting of common and distinctive features enables the model to account for effects of directionality on similarity judgments. Quite often, the judged similarity of a to b differs from the judged similarity of b to a, as in *Canada is like the United States* and *the United States is like Canada*. For most Americans, Canada is more similar to the United States than the United States is to Canada. Tversky attributes such asymmetries to the differential salience of the features of a and b.[1]

In statements of the form *a is like b*, a is considered to be the topic and b a comment on the topic. The topic-comment distinction is a more general form of the given-new convention. Normally, the subject of a comparison is considered the given information, and the predicate is the source of new information (Clark & Haviland, 1977). This discourse convention leads people to focus on the subject of a comparison. The contrast model incorporates this convention by assigning more weight to the features of the subject than to the features of the predicate. Thus, in the equation for $s(a,b)$, α is usually greater than β. Whenever $\alpha > \beta$, the perceived similarity will be reduced more by the distinctive features of the subject, a, than by the distinctive features of the predicate, b. This means that if a subject is more salient than a predicate, then the similarity of a to b will be greater than the similarity of b to a, as in the Canada-United States example. For most Americans, the United States is the prototype of English-speaking North American countries, and Canada is a variant of that prototype. Because prototypes are more salient than their variants, the variant will always be more similar to the prototype than vice versa (Tversky, 1977).

This formulation seems to work for at least some literal comparisons, but it encounters serious difficulties when applied to metaphorical comparisons. The first difficulty stems from the situation where there are no relevant distinctive features to enter into the equation for perceived similarity. When there are no relevant distinctive features, then the formula for perceived similarity reduces to

$$s(a,b) = \theta \ (A \cap B)$$

where perceived similarity is solely a function of the number of features in common, multiplied by the appropriate weight, θ. In this case, there is no mechanism for similarity to be affected by the direction of comparison. Thus, without any contribution of distinctive features, the perceived similarity of a and b will be the same regardless of direction. For most metaphorical comparisons, such as *my job is like a jail*, a limited set of shared features would be highly salient, but the distinctive features of the two objects—*my job* and *jail*—should be irrelevant. Because irrelevant features are not included in the set of selected features, there will be no distinctive features in the comparison equation. This means that the reversed simile, *a jail is like my job*, would be judged as equivalent to the original. Obviously, it is equivalent neither in meaning nor in perceived similarity.

One way to deal with this problem is to assume that the direction of a comparison can have substantial effects at the very first stages of comprehension, when relevant features are selected. Recall that Tversky accounted for asymmetry in comparison statements by assigning differential salience and weighting to the (preselected) distinctive features of subjects and predicates. For metaphorical comparisons, and for many literal comparisons as well, asymmetries are often produced by differential feature selection. The comprehension process itself can yield different features to be used in similarity judgments, depending on the direction of the comparison. Consider the literal comparisons *Canada is like the United States* and *the United States is like Canada*. The features of the United States attributed to Canada in the first comparison may well be different from the features of Canada that are attributed to the United States in the second. In the former, prototypical features of the United States would be likely candidates: a traditionally English-speaking population in an industrial democratic society with common Anglo-Saxon backgrounds and similar periods of migration are some features that might come to mind. In the latter comparison, the features that might come to mind would be those that are more typical and salient for Canada than for the United States. The issue of a linguistic minority is salient in Canada, particularly in Quebec. Asserting that the United States is like Canada would be one way to say that the United States also has such issues to deal with. These examples are consistent with Grice's maxim of informativeness and with the given-new convention. New information is provided by the predicate to be applied to the subject of the comparison.

Metaphoric comparisons provide the extreme case of asymmetry. Metaphors are not just asymmetrical; they are nonreversible (Glucksberg, McGlone, & Manfredi, 1997). The clearest examples of nonreversibility are provided by assertions that become anomalous when reversed.[2] For example, *alcohol is like a crutch* becomes uninterpretable when reversed (*a crutch is like alcohol*). Other metaphors display nonreversibility by conveying a completely different meaning when reversed. *My surgeon was like a butcher* exemplifies this second case. In its original order, gross incompetence is attributed to that surgeon. When the subject and predicate are interchanged, then it becomes a positive comment on a butcher's skill. *My butcher is a surgeon* would be taken to mean that the butcher cuts meat with skill and precision.[3]

If completely different features can be selected when comparisons are reversed, as in the surgeon-butcher example, then the asymmetry of both literal and metaphoric comparisons can be adequately accounted for by the feature-contrast model of similarity assessment. With this elaboration, then, Tversky's contrast model seems to apply as easily to metaphorical comparison statements as to literal ones. Both kinds require prior extraction of relevant features, and both require context-contingent selection as well as context-contingent weighting of shared features and distinctive features.

There are, however, at least two phenomena that remain untouched by this account. The first is that metaphoric comparisons, unlike literal comparisons, are nonreversible. Although the contrast model can be elaborated to deal with this difference between literal and metaphorical comparisons, it provides no principled reason for the difference. Why are metaphoric comparisons nonreversible?

The second set of phenomena that poses a problem for the contrast model are judgments of metaphoricity itself. People are quite skilled at judging whether a comparison is literal or metaphorical. People can also judge degrees of metaphoricity. For example, *John's face was like a beet* is judged as more metaphorical than *John's face was red like a beet*. As this example illustrates, specifying the dimension or grounds for a comparison reduces perceived metaphoricity (Ortony, 1979). What cues do people use to recognize a comparison as metaphorical and to judge degrees of metaphoricity?

Ortony (1979) developed a modification of Tversky's contrast model to provide a measure of similarity that would be sensitive to metaphoricity. This modification takes advantage of the relative salience of the features that are involved in a comparison. Ortony considers salience imbalance to be the principal source of judgments of metaphoricity. Ortony, Vondruska, Foss, and Jones (1985) also claim that the salience imbalance model can be extended to be a model of comprehension: "Additional assumptions can easily be incorporated to try to account for the comprehension process" (p. 588) as well as to the process of assessing kind and degree of similarity.

Metaphor as Implicit Simile: Salience Imbalance

The salience imbalance model of metaphoric similarity belongs to a class of comprehension models that we will refer to as matching models. Matching models of metaphor comprehension assume that the topic and the vehicle of nominal metaphors (of the form *a noun is [like] a noun*) can be represented either as sets of features or by their positions in a geometric semantic space (see, for example, Johnson & Malgady, 1979; Tourangeau & Sternberg, 1981; Marschark, Katz, & Paivio, 1983; For detailed critiques of matching models in general see Camac & Glucksberg, 1984; Glucksberg, McGlone, & Manfredi, 1997).

Irrespective of specific representation assumptions, matching models of metaphor comprehension assume that metaphors are first recognized as comparison statements; the features or attributes of the vehicle are then compared to, or mapped onto, the features of the topic. The simple forms of such models fail miserably because they cannot account for two of the most salient characteristics of comparison statements, be they literal or metaphorical: (a) selection of relevant features and (b) the asymmetry of directional comparisons. Tversky's contrast model acknowledges these two phenomena by assuming that feature selection is a necessary precondition of the similarity judgment process and by allowing for a focus upon the topic of a comparison. This focus, in turn, is motivated by the convention for marking given and new information (Clark & Haviland, 1977).

Ortony (1979) elaborated the contrast model to deal with two additional phenomena. Tversky's original model does not deal adequately with the irreversibility of metaphoric comparisons. In particular, there is no reason to expect that reversing a comparison would result in an anomalous state- ment. Second, the contrast model is silent with respect to metaphor rec- ognition in the first place. What cues do people use to discriminate between literal and metaphoric comparisons? Ortony's solution to these two prob- lems involves two modifications of the contrast model. First, the salience, or weight, of the matching properties is made to be dependent on the salience value of the matching properties in b, and so Tversky's original equation is rewritten as:

$$s(a,b) = \theta \, f^B(A \cap B) - \alpha \, f^A(A - B) - \beta \, f^B(B - A)$$

where f^A and f^B represent the salience of those properties in the objects a and b respectively. In literal similarity statements such as *copper is like tin*, the properties of b (*tin*) that match with those of a (*copper*) are highly salient in b and in a (high A/high B), so objects a and b will be judged as highly similar. When comparisons involve properties that are of rela- tively low salience in both objects (low A/low B), then those objects will be judged as less similar, as in *Olives are like cherries* (e.g., both olives and cherries have pits). Such statements are trivial and anomalous because they violate Grice's (1975) cooperative principle—they are not informative.[4]

In contrast to such literal comparisons, metaphoric comparisons seem to involve two objects that do not share any salient properties. Instead, the grounds for the comparison involve properties that are highly salient for the vehicle (the b term) but not at all salient for the topic (the a term), as in *sermons are like sleeping pills*. The sleep-inducing properties of *sleeping pills* are central to that concept. These properties are neither salient nor central to the concept *sermons* but can be considered a diagnostic property of at least some subset of that category. Comparison statements that involve this kind of match (low A/high B) are considered to be metaphorical, that is, they are similes. Ortony considers this low-high salience imbalance to be the principal source of metaphoricity, as well as the cue that people use to distinguish among differing degrees of metaphoricity.

Ortony's argument also accounts for the nonreversibility of metaphoric comparisons. Reversed metaphoric comparisons involve properties that are high-salient for the topic and low for the vehicle (high A/low B), as in *sleeping pills are like sermons.* Here, the property of inducing drowsiness seems to be the only plausible similarity between the two concepts. This property, however, is salient for the topic of the statement, *sleeping pills,* but not for the vehicle, *sermons.* Therefore it cannot be used as the "new" information, because, according to the given-new principle (Clark & Haviland, 1977), the topic provides the old or given information. The predicate, *sermons,* has no salient property that can plausibly be attributed to that topic, *sleeping pills* (see Gildea & Glucksberg, 1983; Ortony et al., 1985). Following the reasoning in connection with trivial literal comparison statements (as in the olives-cherries example), reversed similes are also anomalous because they too are uninformative.

This formulation reveals a fundamental flaw in the salience imbalance hypothesis. As Ortony (1979, p. 165) suggests, informativeness is a necessary condition for an acceptable descriptive comparison statement. If a statement is not informative, then it is considered to be anomalous and uninterpretable. Consider now the hallmark of literal comparison statements according to the imbalance model: they involve a high A/high B match. In order for such a statement to be informative, it may involve a high-high match for the speaker, and it may also involve a high-high match for an overhearer who already knows the properties of a and b. It cannot, however, be a high-high match for a listener and still be an informative statement.[5] It follows that all informative comparison statements involve a low A/high B attribution. Some salient property or properties of b are attributed to a. This is as true of literal comparison statements as it is of metaphorical ones. Therefore, salience imbalance cannot distinguish between literal and metaphorical comparisons because such imbalance characterizes all informative comparisons.

This principled failure of the salience imbalance hypothesis is sufficient to reject it as a basis for a model of comprehension. But there is an even more fundamental problem that applies to matching models in general. As Ortony (1979) noted, many metaphoric comparisons seem to involve properties that are not part of the listener's knowledge of the topic at all *until the metaphor is uttered and understood.* Ortony referred to this as property introduction, and it occurs whenever a listener is told something brand new about the subject of a comparison, as in *Roger is like a pit bull in faculty meetings.* The properties of *pit bull* in this context were never part of the listener's mental representation of *Roger.* If comprehension involves a search for matching properties, then it could never succeed in this case.

It clearly can succeed, and so we must abandon a simple matching mechanism in favor of a property attribution strategy (Tourangeau & Sternberg, 1981; Camac & Glucksberg, 1984; Ortony et al., 1985; Glucksberg & Keysar, 1990; Gentner & Wolff, 1997; Glucksberg, McGlone, & Manfredi, 1997).

This consideration suggests that matching models in general cannot account for comprehension of either metaphoric or literal similarity statements. Ortony's argument concerning property introduction applies with equal force to the two kinds of similarity statements. If I know nothing about copper, then telling me that it is like tin introduces properties to my mental representation of the concept *copper*. Informative literal comparisons, therefore, also cannot be based on a successful search for matching properties. Instead, as Ortony astutely argued, they must be based on the recognition of salient and relevant properties of a predicate that can sensibly or plausibly be attributed to the subject of the comparison. Pure matching models, then, may serve as models of comparison-statement *assessment or verification*. They cannot serve as the basis for models of how people interpret such statements, be they literal or metaphorical, unless they are elaborated to deal with the issues raised here.

Metaphors as Implicit Similes: Structural Alignment

Gentner and Wolff (1997) recognize that pure matching models fail to capture important metaphoric phenomena, as originally argued by Glucksberg and Keysar (1990, 1993). We have already discussed the feature selection problem, a problem recognized by matching theorists but either finessed or inadequately addressed (e.g., Tversky, 1977; Ortony, 1979). A second problem is how features are matched. In metaphoric comparisons such as *men are like wolves* and *my lawyer is like a shark*, the way in which wolves are predators is different from the way men are predators, which in turn is different from the way sharks are predators and lawyers are predators. How similar but nonidentical properties might be matched is not a trivial problem (Black, 1962, 1979; Way, 1991). One approach would be to match on the basis of similarity rather than identity. This, however, would require a procedure to determine similarity of features prior to determining similarity of objects. Unfortunately, this can lead to an infinite regress (Gentner, 1983).

Gentner and her colleagues have developed a structural alignment model of metaphor comprehension that, in principle, deals with many of the problems that we have identified for pure matching models: feature selection, attribution of new features to metaphor topics, nonreversibility of metaphoric comparisons, and matching of nonidentical features. Two problems that are not addressed are how metaphoric comparisons are identified as such and the ability to paraphrase metaphoric comparisons as metaphors and vice versa (e.g., statements of the form *A is like B* can always be paraphrased as *A is B*). We return to these two issues after we outline Gentner's structural alignment model of metaphor interpretation.

The model initially bypasses the feature selection problem. Interpretation begins by aligning the representations of the topic and the vehicle. Once the two representations are aligned, then all identical features in the topic and the vehicle representations are matched. A significant property of the model is that not only features but relations between features are matched. Thus, for the simile *Tree trunks are like straws*, the matching operation would begin by linking the relations that are common to tree trunks and straws. One relation in common is TRANSPORT. Tree trunks transport water from the ground to its branches; straws transport water from a container to the mouth. Nonidentical features are then linked if they play the same roles in identical relations. In this way, nonidentical but similar features can now be matched (e.g., *branches* would be matched with *mouth*, and *sap* could be matched with *milk* or any other beverage). This solves the problem of matching similar but nonidentical features. Similarity is established in terms of relational functions.

The second and third stages provide mechanisms for feature selection and feature introduction. In the second stage, local matches are collected to form "structurally consistent connected clusters." Features that cannot be connected in terms of structural relations are dropped out, leaving only potentially relevant features for the third stage, where the clusters are themselves merged to form one or more "maximal structurally consistent interpretations" (Gentner & Wolff, 1997, pp. 334–335). If there is more than one such interpretation, then the most systematic and context-appropriate interpretation(s) is chosen. Each interpretation, whether finally chosen or not, follows the given–new convention. That is, candidate inferences are drawn from the vehicle to the topic, but not vice versa. These aspects of the model permit (a) property introduction where matches are not available and (b) directionality, because inferences are always drawn from the vehicle to the topic, and never vice versa (Bowdle & Gentner, 1997).

Beyond Similarity: Metaphors Are Understood Directly

The structural alignment model, as elaborated by Gentner and her colleagues, overcomes many of the shortcomings of pure matching models. However, it does not explicitly address the question that originally stimulated Ortony's salience imbalance proposal: what distinguishes metaphoric comparisons from literal ones?[6] One clear difference is the availability of the class-inclusion construction for metaphoric, but not literal, comparisons. In this respect, metaphoric resemblance is clearly not the same as literal resemblance. The *Webster Dictionary* defines simile as "a figure of speech comparing two unlike things," as in *My job is like a jail*. Literal resemblance, in contrast, is between two like things, as in *Copper is like tin*. This produces an intriguing paradox. Metaphoric comparison statements involving two unlike things can easily be paraphrased to look like class inclusion statements, as in *My job IS a jail*. Similarly, *Sermons are like sleeping pills* can be expressed as *Sermons ARE sleeping pills*. In contrast, literal statements that compare two like things cannot be paraphrased as class inclusion statements: *Bees are like hornets* becomes false if expressed as *Bees are hornets*. This difference between metaphoric and literal comparisons may provide the clue to an essential difference between them. Literal comparisons always involve two objects at the same level of abstraction: they typically belong to the same category. Tin and copper are both metals; bees and hornets are both insects. Indeed, literal comparisons may be understood by casting the concepts being compared into a common category. For example, when asked how lemons and oranges are alike, people usually respond that they are both citrus fruits. [7] When a comparison is intended to provide new information, as in *ugli fruit is like an orange*, people may infer that the superordinate category exemplified by the predicate, *orange*, constitutes the relevant grounds of the comparison. Once the citrus fruit category is inferred, then properties of this category (e.g., pulpy juicy flesh, tangy taste, lots of Vitamin C) can be attributed to the unfamiliar *ugli fruit*.[8]

Metaphoric comparisons can be understood in essentially the same way. The statement *Yeltsin was a walking time bomb* can be interpreted as an assertion that the former President of Russia[9] belonged to a category that is exemplified by time bombs. Of the several categories that time bombs could exemplify, only those that may plausibly contain a government leader would be considered for interpretation purposes. Thus, although time bombs could exemplify weapons used by terrorists and assassins, this category would not be considered because it cannot normally include people as members. A head of state may indeed be a terrorist but could not plausibly be a terrorist's weapon. Time bombs can also exemplify the more abstract category of "things that explode at some unpredictable time in the future and cause a lot of damage." Regrettably, perhaps, this category can include heads of state as members. Perhaps metaphoric comparisons are typically understood in terms of such abstract categories. How should such categories be named?

How Novel Categories Are Named: Dual Reference

As we have seen, *time bomb* can be used to refer at two different levels of abstraction. At the basic, concrete level, it refers to an explosive device that will go off at some time in the future. At the superordinate level, it refers to an abstract category that has the essential properties of time bombs—that they cause damage at some unpredictable future time. Why do people use the name for one thing as the name for another (e.g., the name for actual explosive devices as the name for some thing or person that will erupt in some way at some time in the future)? There is a group of natural languages in which superordinate categories do not normally have names of their own. These languages have solved the problem of how to refer to categories that, in any particular language, are not lexicalized (i.e., do not have a single-word name).

American Sign Language (ASL) is one of the many natural languages that, in general, do not have names for superordinate categories. In ASL, basic-level objects have primary signs that are strictly analogous to mon-olexemic English names such as *chair*, *table*, and *bed*. Unlike English, however, ASL has no single-word name for the superordinate category *furniture*. Does this mean that ASL signers cannot refer to this category? Certainly not. *Furniture* in ASL can be referred to by using basic-object signs that are prototypical of that category, as in *house-fire [+] lose all chair-table-bed, etc., but one left, bed*. In English, this could be expressed as *I lost my furniture in the house fire, but one thing was left, the bed* (Newport & Bellugi, 1978, p. 62). The sequence *chair-table-bed-etc.* is signed rapidly with the et cetera sign crisply executed, unlike that same sequence when used to list or enumerate three separate entities. In addition, signing *one left, bed* to complete the assertion makes clear that the sign for bed has a dual reference function. It is used to refer to two different things. The first *bed* is used as part of the name for *furniture*, the second as the name for the individual object, *bed*.

ASL belongs to the group of languages called classifier languages. Like ASL, these languages do not normally have names for superordinate categories, and they too employ the strategy of dual reference to refer to such categories.[10] In Burmese, for example, "nouns can appear in the classifier slot as well as in the noun slot—this repeater construction . . . provides a way in which *the noun can carry out its own function and that of the classifier it replaces*" (Denny, 1986, p. 304, emphasis added). Furthermore, "when a classifier is used in conjunction with a full noun, it is usually highly pro-totpyical" (Craig, 1986, p. 8). Closer to home, some of the Native American Languages spoken in the southwestern United States typically use prototypical category member names as names for the superordinate category itself. In Hopi, for example, the name of the most abundant decid-uous tree, *cottonwood*, is also used as the name for the category of decid-uous trees (Trager, 1936–1939). Similarly, the word for *eagle* is used by Shoshoni speakers to refer to large birds in general (Hage & Miller, 1976). Occasionally, to avoid ambiguity, a more specific term is introduced. For example, the Kiowa speakers in western Oklahoma use *cottonwood* for trees in general, and *real-cottonwood* for the specific tree (Trager, 1936–1939). In each of these cases, the principle is clear. The name of a prototypical category member can be used to name a category that has no name of its own.

In these examples, the lack of category names stems from a design feature of the language itself. Classifier languages generally do not have individual monolexemic terms for superordinate categories. In languages that do have superordinate category names, such as Hebrew or English, there are occasional—perhaps more than occasional—categories that do not have their own names, either because they are new and have not yet been named or for some other reason that may not be apparent. A striking example of a new category that received its name from one of its proto-typical members was reported in a newspaper article about the war crimes trial of John Demjanjuk. Demjanjuk had been accused of being "Ivan the Terrible," a cruel and sadistic prison guard at the Treblinka death camp in Poland during World War II. He was living in the United States at the time of the newspaper article and was later extradited to stand trial in Israel. A conversation between a native Israeli and an American reporter reveals a typical instance of dual reference (emphases added):

Israeli: "If he is *a Demjanjuk*, then he should be condemned to death."
Reporter: "But he is Demjanjuk, his name is John Demjanjuk."
Israeli: "I know his name is Demjanjuk, but I don't know if he is *a Demjanjuk*."

As the newspaper article pointed out, the term *Demjanjuk* was used in this conversation in two ways: to refer to the person John Demjanjuk and also to refer to the category of people that he exemplified, *a Demjanjuk*: "The name Demjanjuk has become a noun in Israel, a word to identify *an ordinary person capable of committing unspeakable acts*" (Shinoff, 1987, emphasis added). As it turned out, John Demjanjuk was found not guilty and has since applied for permission to return to the United States. It would be quite apropos to assert, in this context, that John Demjanjuk was not *a Demjanjuk* after all!

More mundane examples abound. Perhaps the most mundane are brand names that are used to name the category of products that they have come to exemplify: *Kleenex* for facial tissues in general, *Jeep* for all-purpose four-wheel drive vehicles, *Xerox* machine for dry-paper copiers, and *Jell-O* for gelatin desserts. These brand names are used both in their generic and in their specific senses. Because such names can be used both at the basic level and at the superordinate level, they, like metaphors, can be used interchangeably in comparison and in categorical assertions. One could say that *Scotties are Kleenex* or *Scotties are like Kleenex*[11] in the same way that one could say *My lawyer is a shark* or *My lawyer is like a shark*.

The relations among the various potential referents of metaphor vehicles such as *shark* are illustrated in the following list. Just as everything in the world is similar to everything else in the world in some way (Goodman, 1972), so can anything in the world be classified in any number of ways (Barsalou, 1983). *Shark*, for example, may belong to an indefinite number of categories. *Shark* can be a barbecue ingredient, along with tuna and salmon. As such, it is a member of a more general category, *seafood*, to be grouped with flounder, halibut, sardines, and lobster. Because shark and salmon can belong to a common category, they are similar to each other. Shark is like salmon in the context of foods for outdoor grilling. *Shark* can also be a marine predator, along with barracuda and killer whales. In this context, sharks are like barracuda. Even more generally, *shark* can be a vicious predator and be grouped with lions, tigers, hawks and eagles. In this context, sharks are like eagles. The general principle is that when two objects can be sensibly grouped into a single category, then they can resemble each other precisely with respect to the salient characteristics of that category.

Hypothetical Representation

Metaphorical Shark	*Literal Shark*
Vicious	Vicious
Predatory	Predatory
Aggressive	Aggressive
Tenacious	Tenacious
	Can Swim
	Has Fins
	Has Sharp Teeth
	Has Leathery Skin
	Has Gills

Shark can also belong to categories that do not have conventional names of their own. One such category is the set of entities that share a number of related properties. They are swift, powerful, relentless, voracious, and predatory, they have neither conscience nor compassion, and they strike fear into the hearts of their intended victims. Other members of this category could be entities such as *lawyers*. Just as *sharks* can belong to an indefinite number of categories, so can *lawyers*. Lawyers can be adults, human beings, well-paid professionals, academics, members of prestigious firms, charlatans, prosecutors, judges, contentious nitpickers, people who defend the powerless, and so on. These category assignments seem "literal." Somewhat less literal, perhaps, is the category assignment that places *some lawyers* into the same category as *sharks*. What shall that category be called? Because that category has no name of its own, the name of a prototypical member of that category can be used, namely *shark*. Thus, although some lawyers may be civil, gentle, scholarly, and kind, others may be vicious and could even be described as *literally out for blood*. These kinds of lawyers are not only like sharks; they *are* "sharks."

The relation between categorical and comparison statements is now clear. In the comparison form *my lawyer is like a shark*, *shark* is used to refer to the marine creature. In categorical form, *my lawyer is a shark*, *shark* is used to refer to the more abstract category of predatory entities (see the above list). When such a category is used to characterize a metaphor topic, it functions as an attributive category in that it provides properties to be attributed to the topic. With extensive and repeated use, the attributive category that is exemplified by a vehicle may become part of a term's conventional meaning. When this happens in a language community, heretofore nonlexicalized categories, such as *disastrous military interventions*, become lexicalized, as in *Cambodia has become Vietnam's Vietnam*. In this statement, the dual reference function of the term *Vietnam* is explicit. The term occurs twice, and its intended referent on the first occasion is different from its intended referent on the second occasion. On the first occasion it refers to the country itself; on the second it refers metaphorically to the category of disastrous military interventions that the Vietnam war has come to exemplify and symbolize. The difference between these two uses of *Vietnam* is analogous to the difference between the two uses of *Demjanjuk*: to name a particular entity and to refer to a category of entities with certain characteristics in common. As Roger Brown put it, "Metaphor differs from other superordinate-subordinate relationships in that the superordinate is not given a name of its own. Instead, the name of one subordinate [i.e., the vehicle] is extended to the other" (1958b, p. 140).[12]

This formulation helps to account for two of the several phenomena untouched by the metaphor-as-comparison view: the reason metaphors can be paraphrased as similes and vice versa, and the basis for people's ability to judge whether a statement is intended literally or metaphorically.

Structure of Attributive Metaphor Categories

Commonplace natural kind categories display two sets of structural properties, one vertical, the other horizontal (Rosch, 1973, 1978). The vertical property refers to different levels of abstraction. The category *food*, for example, is organized hierarchically, from the superordinate *food* to *vegetable*, which is superordinate to *salad greens*, which is superordinate to *lettuce*, which in turn is superordinate to *iceberg lettuce*. In this taxonomy, *salad greens*, *lettuce*, and *iceberg lettuce* can be considered as superordinate, basic, and subordinate level terms, respectively.[13]

Metaphoric and other functional categories are also hierarchically organized. Consider the functional category *foods to eat on a diet to lose weight*. When people are asked to provide examples for such ad hoc categories, a hierarchical structure emerges (Barsalou, 1983). For the general category *diet foods*, *salad greens* would be at the superordinate level, *lettuce* at the basic level, and *romaine lettuce* at the subordinate level.[14] The relative positions of terms within such hierarchical categories determines when comparisons are permissible and when categorical assertions are permissible. In general, comparisons are restricted to terms that refer at the same level of abstraction. Thus, we can have comparisons between superordinates, as in *fresh fruits are like salad greens*, but not between superordinates and subordinates within a category, as in *lettuce is like salad greens* or *romaine lettuce is like lettuce*. When two entities are at different levels in a taxonomic hierarchy, then the appropriate relation is categorical, not one of similitude, as in *lettuce is a salad green* or *romaine is a (kind of) lettuce*.

Metaphorical attributive categories are functional categories that also display a hierarchical organization. The category of vicious, predatory beings, even though having no name of its own, is organized in terms of superordinate and subordinate levels. The marine creature *shark* is at the basic level, *tiger shark* at the subordinate level, and *predatory, vicious, tenacious, etc., creatures* is at the superordinate level. Likening my lawyer to a shark places *my lawyer* at the basic level, together with the literal shark. Saying that my lawyer *is* a shark places *shark* at the superordinate level, where it is used as the name for that superordinate category of predatory beings. As noted earlier, this use of the term *shark* is analogous to the use of prototypical category member names as superordinate level names in classifier languages such as ASL (Newport & Bellugi, 1978; Suppalla, 1986).

Functional categories also have the same horizontal structure as ordinary taxonomic categories. For any given category, some members are more typical than others: they would be considered the "ideal" examples of a category (Barsalou, 1985). In the *vegetable* category, for example, people agree that *green beans* and *carrots* are prototypical vegetables, *olives* less so. When asked whether *green beans* or *carrots* are vegetables, people consistently agree that they are. When asked whether *olives* or *peanuts* are vegetables, people are much less consistent, sometimes saying yes, sometimes no (McCloskey & Glucksberg, 1978). Functional categories also have graded category membership. In the category of diet foods, *yogurt* would be typical, *egg whites* less so. Similarly, in the category of predatory creatures, *shark* would be typical, *barracuda* less typical, and *swordfish* even less so.[15]

Attributive categories such as *shark* that exemplify a set of properties can be used to attribute those properties to appropriate topics of interest, such as *my lawyer*. Such categories may pre-exist in the form of conventional metaphors, and so they can have conventional names. One such pre-existing category is *butcher*, as used in expressions of the form *X is a butcher*, when *X* is not literally a person who cuts and sells meat but instead is anyone who is grossly incompetent or is exceptionally murderous. The categorical assertion that *my surgeon was a butcher* assigns *my surgeon* to the class of people who are incompetent and who grossly botch their job. That this category, *butchers*, has become conventional in contemporary English can be seen in our dictionaries: one sense of the word *butcher* is "one who bungles something" (*American Heritage Dictionary*, 1992, p. 261).

But such categories need not pre-exist. They can be created on the fly to accomplish communicative aims, as in expressions such as *my accountant is a spreadsheet*. The category *spreadsheet* can be created to attribute certain properties to the metaphor topic *my accountant*. This category, even though created *de novo*, has the same structural organization as ordinary taxonomic categories. They are organized in hierarchical levels, and so one can be more general and say that *my accountant is a walking database* or be more specific and say that *my accountant is a Lotus Spread Sheet*. They also have members that vary in typicality. A *spreadsheet* exemplifies orderly arrays of data; a *table of numbers* might denote the same sort of thing, but it is not the ideal. In general, metaphors are most apt when ideal exemplars—prototypical category members—are used.[16]

And, like any other functional category, metaphorical attributive categories are partly retrieved from memory and partly constructed as needed. As Barsalou (1987) put it, "Rather than being retrieved as static units from memory to represent categories, concepts originate in a highly flexible process that retrieves generic information and episodic information from long term memory to construct temporary concepts in working memory. . . . [T]his concept construction process is highly constrained by goals . . . [and] contexts" (p. 101).

Even with conventional metaphors, context guides and constrains concept construction, that is, interpretation. Consider the conventional metaphor *X is a gold mine*. Without further specification of *X*, *gold mine* can be interpreted only in general terms, as some entity that is valuable in some way. Once *X* is specified, then the concept of *gold mine* can also be specified. If *X* is *a library*, then the concept of *gold mine* is instantiated as a place with a wealth of information in the form of books and other reference materials. If *X* is an invention, then *gold mine* is taken to mean something that will earn the inventor a great deal of money. And, of course, if *X* is a hole in the ground, then *gold mine* is not a metaphorical concept at all.

Metaphor as Class Inclusion: Some Implications

If metaphors are exactly what they look like—class-inclusion assertions—then the metaphor phenomena that we were concerned with can be naturally accounted for. The phenomena of interest include:

1. Nonreversibility of metaphors, and why metaphors can be paraphrased as similes and vice versa.
2. Judgments of metaphoricity, including the effects of hedges on perceived metaphoricity.
3. How literally true assertions can still be metaphors (e.g., *people are not sheep*, although literally true, can still convey metaphorical meaning beyond their literal interpretation).
4. What makes a metaphor more or less apt.
5. How verbs can be used metaphorically, as in *The dog flew across the yard in pursuit of the intruder.*

We briefly examine each of these issues in turn.

Are Metaphors Ever Reversible?

Class-inclusion assertions are nonreversible. One can say that *a tree is a plant*, but the reverse, *a plant is a tree*, is anomalous. Metaphoric comparisons behave in exactly the same way: *sermons are like sleeping pills* makes sense, but *sleeping pills are like sermons* does not. This follows from the argument that metaphoric comparisons—similes—are implicit class-inclusion assertions. Thus, just as literal class-inclusion assertions are, in principle, nonreversible, so are metaphorical class-inclusion assertions; *sermons are sleeping pills* makes sense, but *sleeping pills are sermons* does not.

As we noted earlier, when reversed metaphors do make sense, then either of two things has happened. When the interpretation of a reversed metaphor does not change, then people seem to implicitly undo the reversal, as in *a mighty fortress is our God*. When reversing a metaphor changes its interpretation, then it is simply a different metaphor, as in *some surgeons are butchers* and *some butchers are surgeons*. The effects of reversing metaphors were demonstrated by Glucksberg, McGlone, and Manfredi (1997), who asked college students to rate the comprehensibility of metaphors, similes, and literal comparison statements in both their original and reversed orders and then to provide paraphrases of all the statements that were rated as comprehensible. As expected, metaphors and similes were rated as highly comprehensible in their original orders but as far less comprehensible in reversed order (e.g., *their trust is [like] glue* was rated as highly comprehensible, whereas *glue is like their trust* was rated as either incomprehensible or minimally so). Most people couldn't provide any paraphrase at all of this reversed metaphor. Others offered attempts such as "they trust the glue to work," but they were not particularly confident about their interpretations. In contrast, literal comparisons were rated as equally comprehensible regardless of order; for example, *His Ph.D. is like an M.D.* not only was rated equally comprehensible in reversed order but was also paraphrased as meaning pretty much the same thing: both are advanced degrees, requiring the same number of years in school. Comparison theories of metaphor comprehension can, of course, account for the asymmetrical nature of similes in terms of the given-new convention. However, similes are not simply asymmetrical; they are categorically nonreversible. Unlike the class-inclusion view, comparison theories do not provide a principled basis for this categorical irreversibility.

How Are Metaphors Recognized as Such?

The traditional view of how metaphors are recognized falls naturally out of truth-conditional semantics and the standard pragmatic three-stage model of metaphor comprehension. Metaphors are considered to be semantically deviant, and the deviance is used as a signal that an utterance may not be intended literally. For nominal metaphors, the categorical assertion *X is a Y* is recognized as false, and an alternative nonliteral interpretation is then sought, usually in the form of *X is like a Y*. We have already shown that this does not work as a process model, and it is easy to show that semantic deviance—that is, categorical falsehood—does not suffice as a signal for metaphoricity. First, it is not at all difficult to find examples of metaphors that are not literally deviant. Among the more conventional are the literally true assertions *no man is an island* and *people are not sheep.* How do people recognize that these literally true statements are metaphors?

One cue to metaphoricity might be the dual-reference function of the metaphor vehicle. In assertions such as *no man is an island*, people implicitly recognize that the word *island* is used to refer to an abstract category that includes the concrete referent *island* as one if its exemplars. People can also implicitly recognize that the metaphor can be paraphrased into simile form as *no man is like an island* (as awkward as this might seem). The same argument holds for literally false metaphors, such as *my job is a jail*, where the term *jail* can refer to the general category of unpleasant, confining situations, as well as to the concrete brick-and-steel structure that houses prisoners. I suggest that recognition of the dual-reference function of the metaphor vehicle and the recognition that the assertion can be paraphrased as a simile are cues that an utterance might be intended metaphorically.

Dual-reference recognition may thus be a necessary condition for signaling metaphoricity. However, it cannot be sufficient because, as we have seen, dual reference occurs whenever a specific name is used generically, as in *Kleenex* for facial tissues in general. In addition to using dual reference, a good metaphor must also provide salient properties of the category that it exemplifies for attribution to the metaphor topic. In Kleenex-type naming cases, an object is simply identified as a member of a category, without any further characterizations of interest.

Good metaphors, then, are acts of classification that attribute (or deny, in the case of negations) an interrelated set of properties to their topics. It follows that metaphoric comparisons acquire their metaphoricity by behaving as if they were class-inclusion assertions. The assertion that *cigarettes are like time bombs* can be identified as a simile, rather than a literal comparison, by recognizing that it can be paraphrased as *cigarettes are time bombs.* The closer an utterance is to a categorical assertion, the more metaphorical it should be.

The available evidence is consistent with this claim. First, people can reliably judge degrees of metaphoricity. More to the point, the judged metaphoricity of comparison statements is reduced when the statement is hedged, as when a dimension of similarity is made explicit. For example, people judge that *John's face was like a beet* is more metaphorical than *John's face was red like a beet* (Ortony, 1979). The effect of hedges is highly systematic; any weakening of the categorical force of a statement tends to reduce its perceived metaphoricity. This is illustrated in the following statements, arranged in decreasing order of perceived metaphoricity:

1. Cigarettes are literally time bombs.
2. Cigarettes are time bombs.
3. Cigarettes are virtual time bombs.

4. Cigarettes are like time bombs.
5. In certain respects, cigarettes are like time bombs.
6. Cigarettes are deadly, like time bombs.
7. Cigarettes are as deadly as time bombs.

Perhaps paradoxically, using the intensifier *literally* in a metaphor can increase its perceived metaphoricity. Why? One possibility is that it emphasizes the intention to categorize the topic as a member of the category exemplified by the metaphor vehicle. At the other end of the metaphoricity dimension, simply stating that the topic is equivalent to the metaphor vehicle on a particular dimension removes all traces of metaphoricity. Anything that kills can be as deadly as a time bomb, and, without any of the other properties of the category exemplified by time bombs, no sense of metaphoricity is transmitted.

When Can Literally True Assertions Also Be Metaphors?

In a withering retort during a vice presidential campaign debate some years ago, Lloyd Benson said to Dan Quayle, "I know you and I knew John Kennedy, and I can tell your right now, sir, you're no John Kennedy!" Everyone in the audience knew immediately what was intended: not an uninformative statement that Dan Quayle was Dan Quayle and not John Kennedy but that he was not *A* John Kennedy and thus not *like* John Kennedy, either.[17] Consistent with Grice's cooperative principal, utterances are assumed to be relevant and informative. An obvious fact—that Dan Quayle is not John Kennedy, or that people are neither land masses surrounded by water nor four-footed wooly ovines—is not ordinarily taken to be a speaker's intended meaning.

The intended meaning is assumed to be both informative and relevant. This assumption, plus the assumption of dual reference and property attribution, helps us understand how categorical negations can function metaphorically. A positive class-inclusion assertion places a topic of interest into a relevant category and, by so doing, attributes one or more diagnostic properties to that topic. Similarly, a negative class-inclusion assertion excludes a topic of interest from a potentially relevant category and so denies that the topic has certain characteristics. *People are not islands* is an assertion that people are not isolated individuals disconnected from one another. This metaphor expresses a firmly held belief in most human societies that the fate of any one person is connected to the fate of all: "Ask not for whom the bell tolls, it tolls for thee" (John Donne, 1635). Similarly, *people are not sheep* is simply the obverse of *man is a wolf*. These two assertions—one literally true and the other literally false—convey similar meanings—that human nature is not typically docile but instead aggressive and rapacious. Both involve dual reference, both use metaphor vehicles that exemplify their respective attributive categories, and both attribute (or deny) sets of properties relevant to their topics.

What Makes a Metaphor Apt?

Goal-directed ad hoc functional categories have graded structure (Barsalou, 1983). Metaphoric attributive categories, as a special case of functional categories, have graded structure, as well. For example, *gold* is a prototypical member of the category of rare and valuable things. *Platinum*, although more costly and even rarer than gold, is not a typical member of that category; neither are sapphires or silver. Perhaps because of differences in typicality among these four exemplars of valuable things, they also differ in aptness when used as metaphor vehicles; *Not even Einstein's ideas were all gold* seems more apt than *not even Einstein's ideas were all platinum. Silver* and *sapphires* work even less well.

Gold is a conventional metaphor vehicle.[18] Would novel metaphor vehicles also be most apt if they exemplified the category that has just been created de novo? When novel metaphors are coined, this certainly seems to be the case. When Orange County in California almost faced bankruptcy in 1994 because of its disastrous investment policy, it immediately became a metaphor for any governmental unit facing financial ruin. As a *New York Times* headline about New York State's financial situation several months later put it, "Will New York become the next Orange County?" In the realm of politics and scandals, few would deny that the Watergate incident during Nixon's presidency exemplified scandal and wrong doing in high places. Hence the use of *-gate* as a way to name and categorize any other such scandal: Iran-gate, Nanny-gate, and Whitewater-gate, to cite but a few.[19]

In general, prototypical members of metaphorical categories, when used with appropriate topics, should produce highly comprehensible and apt metaphors. In addition, metaphors such as *the wolf is the shark of the forest* are most comprehensible and are judged most apt when the metaphor vehicle, for example, *shark*, is at the extreme of one or more relevant semantic dimensions (Tourangeau & Sternberg, 1981). In this particular metaphor, the dimension is ferocity among predators, and *shark* ideally exemplifies this category.

Similarly, when a metaphor is systematic and has parts that may be functionally relevant to that metaphor, then "good" parts should produce better metaphors than less good parts. Systematic metaphors are conventional in a language community.[20] They are also more complex than the simple nominal metaphors that we have discussed here, but they follow the same principles. For example, to say that a theory's foundation is crumbling implicitly treats *theory* as belonging to the category of *structures*. The specific *structure* category is specified by the exemplar-superordinate relation of *theory* as a type of structure, and it enables people to describe theories in terms of appropriate parts of structures. What parts of a metaphoric category such as *structures* are appropriate?

Parts of objects vary in "goodness" (Tversky & Hemenway, 1984). Good parts are those that are functionally important to the object. The *wing* of an airplane, for example, is a "good" part; the *floor* is not, even though a floor is essential. The concept of part goodness is analogous to the concept of prototypicality of category members. Thus, the goodness of a part is also analogous to the prototypicality of a metaphor vehicle in simple nominal metaphors. This, in turn, suggests that for the systematic metaphor of *theory as a structure*, some parts of structures are better, and hence more apt, than others for describing theories. Specifically, they should be only those parts of structures that are functionally important not only for structures but for theories, as well. The parts *foundation*, *walls*, and *plumbing* might be good parts in that they can be relevant to the integrity or strength of a theory. The parts *chimney*, *roof*, and *corner* are not good because their functional roles in the structure of a theory are not apparent. Analogous to simple nominal metaphors, such parts are irrelevant to the metaphor, just as the fins of a shark are irrelevant to the *lawyer-shark* metaphor.

How Are Verbs Used Metaphorically?

Predicative metaphors use verbs rather than nouns metaphorically, but they function very much as do nominal metaphors (Torreano, 1997). Just as nominal metaphors use vehicles that epitomize certain categories of objects, situations, or events, predicative metaphors use verbs that epitomize certain categories of actions. For example, the verb *to fly* literally entails movement in the air. Flying through the air epitomizes speed, and so expressions such as *he hopped on his bike and flew home* are readily understood via the same strategies by which nominal metaphors, such as *his bike was an arrow*, are understood. Arrows are prototypical members of the category of speeding things; flying is a prototypical member of the category of fast travel. For both nominal and predicative metaphors, prototypical members of categories can be used as metaphors to attribute properties to topics of interest. And, in both cases, the names of prototypical category members are used to name categories that have no names of their own.

How do people recognize when a verb is used metaphorically? We have already seen that nominal metaphors need not be semantically anomalous or false to be perceived as metaphors. Similarly, in predicative metaphors, there need be no semantic or other kind of violation or deviance. Nevertheless, when either nouns or verbs are used metaphorically, either semantic or syntactic principles are often violated. One way to use a verb deviantly is to violate its selection restrictions. Selection restrictions are constraints on a verb's arguments. For example, the verb *to eat* usually requires an animate subject and an edible direct object. *Tom ate the apple* is therefore semantically acceptable. *The desktop printer ate the paper* is not. The former sentence is literally acceptable; the latter can be understood only metaphorically. But, as with nominal metaphors, verbs may also be used in perfectly acceptable ways and still be taken metaphorically (e.g., *after years of fruitless research, the professor woke up to face reality*). The verb *to wake* must have an animate subject, and, despite the occasional soporific lecture, *professor* is still an animate noun. Nonetheless, people take the use of "wake up" in this assertion to be metaphorical. Why is "wake up" in this context judged to be metaphorical?

One cue to metaphoricity is dual reference. When "wake up" is used metaphorically, the literal act of waking up exemplifies any instance of a transition from unawareness to awareness. Because literal waking up exemplifies this category of situations, it can be used as a name for that category. Recognition of this dual-reference role for the verb provides a cue that it is intended metaphorically.

Another cue to verb metaphoricity is analogous to the isa-like paraphrasability of nominal metaphors. Recall that nominal metaphors can always be paraphrased as comparisons, and vice versa. Predicative metaphors can be paraphrased in an analogous way, either as a comparison or as an "as if" statement. For example, the wake-up metaphor could be expressed as *It was as if / it was like the Professor woke up to face reality*. Verbs used literally cannot be paraphrased in this way (e.g., *He woke up at 8:00 A.M. every morning* cannot be paraphrased as *It was as if he woke up at 8:00 A.M. every morning*). This paraphrase actually negates the original assertion. If people implicitly recognize that a verb has dual reference and that the assertion can be paraphrased as an "as if" statement, then this information can be used as a cue to metaphoricity.

Concluding Remarks

We have argued that metaphors are not understood by transforming them into similes. Instead, they are intended as class-inclusion statements and are understood as such. This view provides a principled account of the important metaphor phenomena, including the following:

1. Both nominal and predicative metaphors can be paraphrased as comparison statements, and vice versa. Literal comparisons and literal uses of verbs cannot. This follows directly from the view of metaphoric comparisons as implicit class-inclusion assertions.

2. Statements need not be false or semantically deviant to be perceived as metaphorical. Metaphors can be recognized as such because they involve dual reference and can be implicitly transformed into comparisons.

3. Nominal metaphors are, in principle, nonreversible because they express a class-inclusion relation, and this relation is, by definition, not symmetrical.

4. Hedges and specification of the ground of a metaphor reduce perceived metaphoricity. This follows from the class-inclusion nature of metaphors. The canonical metaphor explicitly expresses an unqualified class-inclusion relation. Anything that weakens the force of a class-inclusion assertion or narrows its scope reduces perceived metaphoricity.

5. Metaphors can vary in aptness. The most apt metaphors are those that use ideal exemplars of their metaphorical categories, provided the topic is appropriate.

Our account of metaphors as categorizations that create new, relevant, and useful characterizations of their topics does not, however, solve the problem of how people come to understand metaphors. What are the specific mechanisms by which people understand both nominal and predicative metaphors? We take up this issue in chapter 4, where we consider a process model of metaphor comprehension: the interactive property attribution model.

Beyond Comparison
Property Attribution

Metaphor brings out the thisness of a that, or the thatness of a this.
Kenneth Burke, 1945

Metaphors work via an interaction between the metaphor vehicle and the metaphor topic. In nominal metaphors, salient properties of the vehicle are attributed to the topic. Thus, in the assertion *her letter was a dagger in his heart*, properties of the vehicle *dagger*, such as piercing, wounding, perhaps even killing, are attributed to the topic, *her letter*. In predicative metaphors, salient characteristics of actions or other verb-referents are attributed to the subject or object of an assertion, as in *consumed by guilt and shame, Fred finally grasped his fate*. In this assertion, Fred is characterized as being either destroyed or totally engrossed (*consumed*)[1] by feelings of shame and guilt and also as fully understanding (*grasping*) what will happen to him. Given that people know the literal meanings of metaphor vehicle terms, how are the intended metaphorical properties of those terms selected? To simplify matters, I will use nominal metaphors to illustrate the workings of the interactive property attribution model and then show how the model applies to predicative metaphors.

As with any model of language comprehension, we need to specify two components of the model: the representational assumptions and the process assumptions. One representational assumption is the dual-reference function of metaphor vehicle terms. A term such as *dagger* simultaneously names the category of piercing, hurtful entities and a prototypical exemplar of that category, real daggers. The second representational assumption concerns the differential roles of metaphor topics and vehicles, enabling them to be used interactively as part of the metaphor comprehension process.

Vehicle Properties and Topic Dimensions

Consider the metaphors *my lawyer was a snake* and *the road was a snake*. *Snake* conveys two different sets of properties in these two metaphors, in each case properties that are relevant to their respective topics. How can a topic be used to select properties that are relevant to it? A topic can be viewed as a local context for the metaphor vehicle. For any given metaphor topic, only certain sorts of property attributions would be context-appropriate, that is, interesting and/or relevant. The relevance of a given property to a topic can best be described in terms of dimensions for attribution. When the topic is *road*, for example, dimensions such as shape (e.g., straight, curved, twisting), surface (smooth or bumpy), and width (narrow or wide), safety, and speed are meaningful and relevant in most contexts in which roads are discussed. Dimensions such as cost (cheap, expensive) and color (black, white, gray) can be meaningful but are irrelevant in most contexts in which roads are discussed. Still other dimensions, such as emotional arousal (calm, neutral, excited) are not normally applicable to roads, and consequently characterizations on these dimensions would usually be meaningless (although twisting mountain roads can be exhilarating). Another way to specify those dimensions that would be meaningful and relevant for a metaphor topic would be to specify the dimensions of within-category variation. For a concept such as *roads*, the ways that roads can differ meaningfully from one another constitute that concept's relevant dimensions for attribution.

The notion of relevant dimensions for attribution is analogous to the notion of relevance as used in the conceptual combination literature (e.g., Murphy, 1988, 1990). When asked to interpret adjective-noun or noun-noun combinations such as *blind lawyer* or *jail job*, existential possibility is often less important than plausibility. For example, people have difficulty interpreting the combination *unframed planet*, even though they readily agree that planets are never framed. This kind of noun phrase is difficult to interpret because the adjective *unframed* does not characterize a dimension that is relevant for the concept *planet*. In terms of within-category variation, the "framing" dimension does not distinguish among members of the category "planets." Other concepts, such as *photograph* or *painting*, may plausibly differ on this dimension, and so the combinations *framed photograph* and *unframed painting* are interpretable. We argue that metaphor topics behave as do head nouns in conceptual combinations: characterizations of topics are meaningful only when they are along relevant attributional dimensions (Wisniewski, 1997).

Our interactive property attribution view of metaphor comprehension thus makes two independent claims. The first claim is that metaphor vehicles and topics play different but interactive roles. A metaphor topic provides dimensions for attribution, while a metaphor vehicle provides properties to be attributed to the topic. Note that this claim does not preclude a comparison process in which information available in the metaphor vehicle is assessed vis-à-vis information available in the metaphor topic. The claim is that the properties per se of the topic and vehicle are not the appropriate inputs to the comparison process. Instead, vehicle properties on the one hand and topic dimensions on the other are the relevant inputs for comparison, analogous to the slots and fillers of head nouns and modifiers in conceptual combinations. The second claim is that the vehicle term can be used to refer at either of two levels of abstraction. When used in the metaphor form *X is a Y*, then it is understood as referring at a higher level of abstraction than the topic term. When a term such as *dagger* is used as a vehicle, it is understood as referring to a superordinate category that includes the topic and the term's literal referent as members. When a vehicle is used in simile form, *X is like a Y*, then it is understood as referring to the subordinate, literal referent.

The two representational assumptions—dual reference of metaphor vehicle terms and differential information made available by topics and vehicles—suggest the following outline of a comprehension process for nominal metaphors. Following the given-new convention, people look for properties of the vehicle to be considered for attribution to the topic. A first step is alignment of the vehicle and the topic concepts so that dimensions for attribution of the topic can be matched against candidate properties of the vehicle. Thus, for a topic such as *dentist*, relevant dimensions such as skill, cost, and availability would be matched with whatever properties are available in a metaphor vehicle. If the vehicle provides properties appropriate for those dimensions, then those would be taken as the grounds for the metaphor. Thus, in the assertion *my dentist was a thief*, the dimensions of skill and cost might be integrated to provide a dimension of value for money, with *thief* providing a specification on that dimension, namely extremely low value. The dentist in question could then be characterized as committing highway robbery. In this example, both topic and vehicle represent near-ideal cases in that the topic *dentist* has a limited number of relevant dimensions and the vehicle *thief* has relatively few but highly salient characteristic properties. But not all topics and vehicles provide such straightforward opportunities for interpretation.

With respect to topics, the number of relevant attributional dimensions varies from topic to topic. Topics with relatively few such dimensions place a high level of constraint on potential attributions. The topic *lawyer*, for example, is likely to be characterized on relatively few dimensions, among them skill, experience, temperament, ambition, reputation, and cost. It would be highly unlikely that any given lawyer would be characterized qua lawyer on dimensions that are irrelevant to the practice of law, such as height, weight, or musical talent. Topics such as *lawyer* thus impose a high level of constraint on potential attributions. In contrast, other topics such as *my brother* provide very few constraints on potential attributions because one might say almost anything about one's brother. Metaphor topics, then, can vary in terms of the level of constraint that they place on interpretation. High-constraining topics produce limited expectations about how they might be characterized, whereas low-constraining topics produce relatively unlimited expectations about how they might be characterized.

Just as topics can vary in the number of relevant attributional dimensions, metaphor vehicles can vary with respect to the number or variety of properties that they can provide as candidate attributions. Some metaphor vehicles are unambiguous in the sense that they uniquely exemplify an attributive category. When used as vehicles, terms such as *shark* and *jail* are relatively unambiguous in this way. *Shark* is emblematic of the category of vicious predators; *jail* is emblematic of situations that are unpleasant and confining. Other metaphor vehicles are relatively ambiguous because they do not uniquely exemplify an attributive category in the ways that *shark* and *jail* do. For example, the phrase *voyage to the bottom of the sea* is an ambiguous metaphor vehicle. Because such a voyage does not exemplify any category in particular, it is unclear what properties this vehicle might provide to characterize a metaphor topic.

The properties of a metaphor vehicle that are attributed to the topic are thus determined by two criteria: (a) the higher-order category (or categories) that the vehicle may exemplify, and (b) whether the prototypical properties of that category characterize the topic in a meaningful way. For example, consider again the metaphors *some roads are snakes* and *some lawyers are snakes*. Different properties of snakes are attributed to the topics *some roads* and *some lawyers*. The attribution of properties in these metaphors is a joint function of the categories that the vehicle can exemplify (e.g., "things with twisting shape" and/or "things that are devious and malevolent") and the relevance constraints imposed by the respective topics (e.g., shape for roads, character for lawyers).

Understanding a metaphor thus requires two kinds of semantic and world knowledge. First, one must know enough about the topic to appreciate which kinds of characterizations are relevant and meaningful (i.e., the relevant dimensions of within-category variation of the topic concept). Second, one must know enough about the metaphor vehicle to know what kinds of things it can epitomize. Given this knowledge base, one can readily understand metaphors with ambiguous vehicles when the metaphor topic is high-constraining (i.e., has relatively few attributional dimensions). Similarly, one can readily understand metaphors with low-constraining topics (i.e., with many attributional dimensions) when the metaphor vehicle is reasonably unambiguous. In this sense, metaphor topics and vehicles are used interactively to generate interpretations.[2]

Differential Roles of Topics and Vehicles

On the interaction view, metaphor topics and vehicles provide different kinds of information to guide interpretations. An empirical test of this view was suggested in a study by Wolff and Gentner (1992). They reasoned that if metaphor topics and vehicles each provide useful information for metaphor comprehension, then providing either the topic or the vehicle in advance of a metaphor itself should facilitate comprehension. Accordingly, they showed people metaphors, one at a time, on a computer screen, with the instruction to press a response key as soon as the participants felt that they understood it. Prior to each metaphor, the topic term, the vehicle term, or a row of x's appeared. As expected, when people knew in advance what the topic or vehicle of a metaphor would be, they understood it faster than they did when they did not have these cues.

We reasoned that only certain kinds of topics and vehicles should be helpful or informative if known in advance. Recall that topics can vary in attributional constraint. High-constraining topics have few attributional dimensions; knowing such a topic in advance of a metaphor should be helpful. In contrast, low-constraining topics have many such dimensions, so knowing the topic in such cases should provide little if any useful information. In terms of Gentner and Wolff's experimental paradigm, high-constraining topics should be effective primes for metaphor understanding, while low-constraining topics should be less so. Similarly, advance knowledge of unambiguous vehicles should be useful for subsequent metaphor processing, but advance knowledge of ambiguous vehicles should not be.[3]

To test these predictions, we used a variant of Wolff & Gentner's priming paradigm with the different types of topics and vehicles as metaphor primes (Glucksberg, McGlone, & Manfredi, 1997). We expected that highly constraining topics would be effective as primes for metaphor comprehension, while low-constraining topics would be either less effective or not effective at all. Analogously, we expected that unambiguous vehicles would be effective primes, while ambiguous vehicles would not. The first step was to construct metaphors with the two kinds of topics and the two kinds of vehicles. To obtain high- and low-constraint topics, we first created a list of candidate items. One example of a high-constraint topic was *memory*; an example of a low-constraint topic was *life*. According to our intuitions, a topic concept such as *memory* is highly constraining about what might be said about it; that is, it can be described in relatively few ways. In contrast, a topic such as *life* places very few constraints about what might be plausibly said about it: *life* can be described in any number of meaningful ways. We also selected a pool of potential metaphor vehicles that were either unambiguous or ambiguous. Unambiguous vehicle terms are those that people agree about: there is consensus about what properties they represent. One example of an unambiguous vehicle is *time bomb*. People agree that *time bomb* epitomizes something that can cause considerable damage at some unpredictable time in the future. In contrast, people disagree about ambiguous vehicles. For example, the concept *garden* does not have a unique set of properties for attribution, so people simply don't agree about what those properties might be.

Before constructing the metaphors for the experiment, we gave all of the candidate topics and vehicles to two groups of college students as a check on our intuitions. The first group rated all of the items in terms of their level of constraint. The students were asked to list, for each item, as many questions as they could think of that would distinguish one instance of the concept from another. We expected that people would list relatively few questions for high-constraint topic concepts and relatively many for the low-constraint ones. The ratings that we obtained were consistent with our initial intuitions. People listed an average of 3.4 questions for high-constraint topics and almost twice as many, 6.2 questions, for low-constraint topics.

To assess vehicle ambiguity, we gave the second group of students the same list of items, but this time in the form *X is a [item]*, with the instruction to consider each sentence frame as a metaphor in which the topic, *X*, had been deleted and to list a property of the deleted *X* term that was implied by the metaphor assertion. For example, for the sentence frame *X is a time bomb*, we expected people to list properties such as *deadly at some future time*. The percentage of people who listed the same property for any given term was our measure of ambiguity; ideally, for the most unambiguous term everyone would list the same property, while ideally, for the most ambiguous term, no two people would agree. In our less-than-ideal real world, the results were more modest but satisfactory none the less. There was 59% agreement, on average, for the unambiguous vehicle terms, and only 21% agreement for the ambiguous terms.[4]

With suitable topics and vehicles in hand, we created forty-eight metaphors. Rather than try to pair high- or low-constraint topics with ambiguous and unambiguous vehicles, we instead chose suitable metaphor vehicles for each of our high- and low-constraint topics and suitable metaphor topics for each of our ambiguous and unambiguous vehicles. We anticipated that all of the metaphors would be equally comprehensible, regardless of topic or vehicle type, because, given an appropriate context, low-constraint topics become constrained and ambiguous vehicles are disambiguated. For example, the low-constraint topic *people* becomes highly constraining in the context of the metaphor *some people are puzzles*. Similarly, the ambiguous vehicle *icebergs* is unambiguous in the context of the metaphor *some offices are icebergs*.

The experimental task was straightforward. College students were asked to read each metaphor when it appeared on a computer screen, one at a time, and to press a key as soon as they felt that they had understood it. Prior to each test item, we gave the students one of three types of prime items. For those metaphors that used the low- or high-constraint topics, the prime was the metaphor itself with the vehicle omitted (e.g., *Some people are *******, followed by the metaphor *Some people are puzzles*). For those metaphors that used the ambiguous and unambiguous vehicles, the prime was the metaphor with the topic deleted (e.g., *Some **** are icebergs*, followed by the metaphor *Some offices are icebergs*). The third prime type was actually not a prime at all but simply the sentence frame *Some **** are ******. The extent to which knowing the topic or knowing the vehicle ahead of time is helpful could now be assessed by comparing the time taken to understand metaphors with each type of prime against the time needed in the no-prime condition.

We first examined the response times for the four metaphor types in the baseline (no-prime) condition. As expected, the four types were equally easy to comprehend.[5] Apparently, low-constraining topics can be constrained by relevant metaphor vehicles, and ambiguous metaphor vehicles can be made unambiguous by relevant topics (see the earlier examples). Because the four metaphor types were comparable in comprehension difficulty, we can now compare the effectiveness of the two types of topic primes and the two types of vehicle primes.

We assessed the priming effects by looking at the differences in comprehension times between baseline (unprimed) and primed conditions for each metaphor type. As expected, priming a metaphor with a topic term or a vehicle term facilitated comprehension, but only if the topic was high constraining or the vehicle was unambiguous. Metaphors preceded by high-constraining topics were understood 35% faster than those in the no-prime condition, while metaphors preceded by low-constraint topics did not benefit significantly (responses were less than 8% faster). Metaphors preceded by unambiguous vehicles profited even more, by 43%, whereas those preceded by ambiguous vehicles were unaffected (comprehension times were about 1% slower than those in the no-prime condition).[6] These data support our claims that (a) level of constraint is an important characteristic of metaphor topics, and (b) degree of ambiguity is an important characteristic of metaphor vehicles.

More broadly, the pattern of priming results is inconsistent with property matching models of metaphor comprehension of the sort proposed by Wolff & Gentner (1992). According to such models, metaphor comprehension begins with an exhaustive extraction of properties of both the topic and the vehicle. After topic and vehicle properties have been extracted, they are then matched against one another. Because matching cannot begin until topic and vehicle properties have been extracted, advance information of the identity of any kind of topic or vehicle should be useful. The sooner the property extraction process is completed, the sooner the subsequent property matching can be accomplished. Thus, advance presentation of *any* metaphor terms should give a head start to the property extraction process and so speed up comprehension. However, we found that advance knowledge of only informative metaphor terms (i.e., high-constraining topics and unambiguous vehicles) was useful for comprehension.

The pattern of priming results is thus most compatible with the interactive property attribution model of metaphor comprehension. More telling, it is a natural outcome of that model. Neither Gentner's (1983) structure mapping model nor Ortony's (1979) salience imbalance model provides a rationale for (a) classifying metaphor topics and vehicles in terms of constraint and ambiguity levels, respectively, or (b) for predicting their differential utility for metaphor comprehension. At the very least, property matching models will need to be elaborated to include the discourse-relevant constructs of topic constraint levels and vehicle ambiguity.

Implicit Metaphors: Conceptual Combinations

The concepts of topic constraint and vehicle ambiguity can be extended to the domain of implicit metaphors, as exemplified in particular kinds of noun-noun combinations. In English, noun-noun combinations, such as *rock star* and *moon rock*, pose problems for interpretation. Unlike languages such as Russian, which have explicit case marking, English provides no explicit information on the roles of the two nouns in such combinations. To compound the problem (pun intended), noun-noun combinations can be interpreted both literally and metaphorically. For example, if the compound *shark lawyer* is interpreted as a lawyer who is predatory and aggressive, then the noun *shark* is used to refer to a metaphorical rather than a literal shark. If the compound is interpreted as a lawyer who represents an environmental group dedicated to protecting sharks from overfishing, then *shark* is used to refer to the literal shark.

In general, noun-noun combinations can be interpreted via any one of three strategies: relational linking, hybridization, and property construction (Wisniewski, 1997). The combination *mourner musician* is typically interpreted via relational linking as meaning a musician who plays for mourners. In such cases, the compound is interpreted in terms of a relation between the head noun (*musician*) and the modifier noun (*mourner*). In hybridization, the two noun concepts are combined so that each acquires properties of the other. *Prose music* might be interpreted via this strategy to mean prose that is sung, as in "Recitative in opera is prose music." Note that in hybridization neither noun can be unambiguously identified as head or modifier because both act as modifier and as modified. In contrast, *medicine music* is typically interpreted via property construction to refer to music that can be used for healing purposes. In such cases, one or more properties of the modifier noun (*medicine*) are attributed to the head noun (*music*). Wisniewski (1996) points out that in many cases of property construction the modifier is used metaphorically rather than literally. One test of whether a modifier noun is being used metaphorically is to follow a procedure used by Levi (1978) to assess adjective-noun combinations. If a noun-noun combination uses the modifier noun metaphorically, then it can be paraphrased as a metaphor of the form *X is a Y*. Thus, the noun-noun combinations *shark lawyer*, *rose girl*, and *movie life* can, if interpreted via property construction, be paraphrased, respectively, as *the lawyer is a shark*, *the girl is a rose*, and *his life is a movie*, respectively. In contrast, neither relational linking nor hybridization interpretations can be paraphrased in this way. *Night snake* (a snake that is active at night) and *heart surgeon* (a surgeon who performs cardiac surgery) cannot be paraphrased as *the snake is a night* or *the surgeon is a heart*. Hybridizations also fail this test. If *robin canary* is taken to mean a cross between a robin and a canary, then the paraphrase *the canary is a robin* does not work. Similarly, if the compound *prose music* is taken to mean prose that is sung or songs that have prose lyrics, then the paraphrase *music is prose* also does not work.

What determines choice of interpretive strategy? Two types of models have been proposed, one patterned after Gentner's structural alignment view (Wisniewski, 1996, 1997), the other after our interactive property attribution view. Wisniewski's model, like many others (e.g., Cohen & Murphy, 1984; Murphy, 1988; Smith, Osherson, Rips, & Keane, 1988; Gagne & Shoben, 1997), assumes a schema representation whereby concepts are represented in terms of dimensions and values (cf. Minsky, 1975; Rumelhart, 1980). For example, the concept *crow* has a color dimension that contains the value *black*. Extending Gentner's (1983) structure-mapping model of analogy and metaphor comprehension, Wisniewski suggests that, in order to comprehend a combined concept, one must initially align the schemas of the two constituent concepts so that the dimensions of one constituent are put into correspondence with analogous dimensions of the other constituent. Once the dimensions are aligned, one then compares the features of the two concepts. This alignment-and-comparison process can be illustrated with the combination *car truck*. In the alignment stage, one aligns dimensions such as the number of wheels, doors, and seats. This alignment permits one to make feature comparisons, from which commonalities and alignable differences may emerge. Both cars and trucks typically have four wheels (a commonality), but cars typically have four doors, whereas trucks have only two, and cars can seat five people, whereas trucks usually seat two (alignable differences). From these alignable differences one could derive the interpretation that a *car truck* is a truck that has four doors and seats five people. Alignable differences are necessary for property interpretation because they indicate (a) what properties to attribute, and (b) the dimensions that they should be attributed to (Wisniewski, 1997). Because people are more likely to find alignable differences for combined concepts with similar constituents than for those with dissimilar constituents (Gentner & Markman, 1994), it follows that property interpretation is more likely for similar combinations. Dissimilar combinations, such as *yarn truck*, have differences, too, but these differences tend to be nonalignable, so their schemas may not coherently be put into correspondence. Thus, because property interpretation requires alignable differences and the differences of dissimilar combinations tend to be nonalignable, property interpretation is unlikely for dissimilar combined concepts. A *yarn truck* likely is not a truck that has properties of yarn but rather a truck that transports yarn. In this way, constituent similarity is seen as the major determinant of interpretation strategy (Wisniewski, 1996, 1997; Wisniewski & Markman, 1993; but see Estes & Glucksberg, 2000a, b, and Wisneiwski, 2000).

To test this hypothesis, Wisniewski (1996) examined people's interpretations of similar (e.g., "shark piranha") and dissimilar (e.g., "shark coconut") combined concepts. As predicted by the alignment-and-comparison model, similar combinations resulted in far more property interpretations (72%) than did relation interpretations (7%). The interpretation of dissimilar combinations, however, was less clear. Nearly half (48%) of these dissimilar combined concepts were understood by property interpretation. These data suggest that constituent similarity may not be necessary for property interpretation.

Other considerations suggest that constituent similarity may be not only unecessary but also insufficient for property interpretations. One determinant of similarity is category membership. In general, two concepts from the same natural or relatively familiar category, such as *small furry animals*, are considered similar.[7] The tendency for similar constituents to be interpreted via property construction, however, poses something of a paradox. In many cases of property construction, the modifier is used metaphorically, as in *medicine music*. However, metaphors by definition involve *dissimilar* constituents. Indeed, rhetoreticians characterize metaphors as two *unlike* things compared, as in *some jobs are jails*. In contrast, literal comparisons involve two *like* things, that is, things that belong to the same taxonomic category (e.g., *wasps are like hornets*). Yet, despite the dissimilarity of the constituents, property construction may often be the preferred strategy for compounds in which the modifier can be understood metaphorically.

A preference for metaphorical property interpretation for dissimilar noun–noun compounds implies that some characteristic(s) other than constituent similarity leads people to interpret such noun–noun compounds via property construction. What might that characteristic be? Interactive property attribution may provide an answer. When a modifier can provide properties that are relevant to a head noun, then property construction should be a likely option. If so, then the interactive property attribution model of metaphor comprehension might be extended as an alternative to the alignment-and-comparison model of noun–noun interpretation.

We assume the same schema system of representation used by alignment-and-comparison models. However, we differ in the details of the initial alignment process. Instead of matching features and seeking alignable differences, we propose that the head and the modifier play the same roles that are played by metaphor topics and vehicles. Like a metaphor topic, the head provides relevant dimensions for attribution. Like a metaphor vehicle, the modifier provides candidate properties for attribution. For example, in the combination *shark lawyer*, the head concept *lawyer* provides relevant dimensions for attribution (e.g., degree of aggressiveness, competence, cost), and the modifier *shark* provides salient candidate properties (e.g., "predatory," "aggressive," and "vicious") that can be attributed. This model, like the alignment-and-comparison model, includes an alignment stage, but it differs in what is aligned. Rather than exhaustively aligning the dimensions and comparing the features of the two concepts, the interactive property attribution model proposes that relevant dimensions of the head are aligned with salient properties of the modifier. According to this model, it is not constituent similarity but rather the interaction of dimensions and features that guides interpretation.

This model seems intuitive and parsimonious for combined concepts such as *zebra clam*. The modifier provides the salient feature "black and white striped," which then fills the color dimension in the head concept. That zebras have hooves and that clams live in the ocean need not be involved in the immediate interpretation process, as alignment-and-comparison models suppose, though this may become important in a secondary elaboration stage (Murphy, 1988).[8]

We can now assess which of the two models of conceptual combination—alignment-and-comparison or interactive attribution—works better by seeing which factors control interpretation strategy. On the alignment-and-comparison view, constituent similarity should be the most important determinant of interpretations: combinations with similar constituents should be interpreted via property construction. Therefore, combinations that are equivalent to one another in constituent similarity should be interpreted via property attribution about the same proportion of the time. In contrast, the interactive attribution model predicts that the relationship between modifier and head nouns is the most important determinant of interpretation strategy. When a compound consists of a head noun with a relevant dimension for attribution and a modifier with a salient property on that dimension, then people should produce property interpretations, irrespective of constituent similarity.

Zachary Estes and I conducted an experiment to test the attribution model (Estes & Glucksberg, 2000). We held the constituent similarity of noun-noun compounds constant while varying the relationship between the modifier and the head nouns. One compound type consisted of modifiers with highly salient features and heads for which those features would be relevant, (e.g., *feather luggage*, where "light" is a salient feature of feathers and "weight" a relevant attribute of luggage. This compound type is high salience-high relevance [HH]). As a control, each of these constituents was also paired with another concept. Gagne and Shoben (1997) noted that many concepts have particular relations associated with them and that people have implicit knowledge of the relative frequencies of these relations. For example, the modifier *feather* might frequently yield an *X is light* interpretation, and this could guide interpretation of *feather X* as an *X that is light*, regardless of what X may be. To control for this possibility, we included a high-salience-low-relevance condition (HL) in which the head did not have a dimension that was relevant to the salient properties of the modifier. To illustrate, although *light* is a salient property of *feather*, the weight dimension is not relevant to the head *storage* in the compound *feather storage*.

Similarly, many concepts have particular dimensions that may invite property attributions from its modifiers. A relevant dimension of *luggage* in most contexts is weight, so the head *luggage* may be given a property attribution on this dimension regardless of the particular modifier. The low salience-high relevance condition (LH) was intended to control for this possibility. This condition consisted of compounds in which the modifier did not have a salient feature that was relevant for that head (e.g., *cotton luggage*). For instance, although the weight dimension is relevant for the head *luggage*, the modifier *cotton* does not have a salient feature on that dimension.

We then had these three types of compounds rated for constituent similarity to ensure that they were in fact equally similar. On a scale of 0 (very dissimilar) to 6 (very similar), the three types of compounds were comparable, ranging from 1.04 to 1.49; that is, they were all at the dissimilar end of the scale. According to the comparison model, all three types should rarely be interpreted via property attribution. According to the interactive property attribution model, the HH compounds should produce a high proportion of property interpretations, while the other two types, with equally dissimilar constituents, should not. For example, because *light* is a salient feature of feathers and *weight* is relevant to luggage, we expected property interpretations for *feather luggage*. But, because *weight* is not relevant to the head noun *storage*, we did not expect property interpretations for *feather storage*. Similarly, although *weight* is relevant to the head noun *luggage*, we expected few property interpretations for *cotton luggage* because *light* is not a salient feature of the modifier *cotton*.

As expected, compounds with the appropriate relation between modifier and head nouns were interpreted via property attribution much more often than the other two compound types. Fully 80% of the high-high compounds were given property interpretations, compared with an average of 20% for the other two types. These results fit very nicely with the preference for metaphorical property interpretations for compounds that are, by definition, dissimilar (cf. Goldvarg & Glucksberg, 1998). The bottom line is that similarity per se is not the controlling factor for interpreting noun-noun compounds, whether the compounds are interpreted literally or metaphorically. Instead, the particular relation between the two noun concepts seems to be paramount. If there is appropriate salience-relevance interaction available, then people will opt for property attribution. If it is not available, then other kinds of interpretations will be generated. More important, the comparison model does not provide any basis for specifying the content of a property interpretation. In contrast, the interactive property attribution model provides a principled basis for specifying the precise properties that will be attributed, not just the idea that some property of the modifier will be attributed to some alignably different dimension of the head concept. The interactive model of metaphor comprehension thus can be extended to the comprehension of attributive noun-noun compounds.

Dual Reference and Levels of Abstraction

The second major claim of the interactive attribution model is that metaphor vehicles can function at two levels of abstraction. In the assertion *some lawyers are like sharks*, for example, the term *shark* can be understood to refer to the literal concept, the marine creature that we call a shark. In the metaphor form, *some lawyers are sharks*, the term *shark* can be understood to refer to the more abstract attributive category of things that the concept *shark* exemplifies, that is, ruthless predators. If this is true, then anything that foregrounds or makes salient the attributive category should facilitate understanding of the metaphor. Conversely, anything that foregrounds or makes salient the literal concrete referent of *shark* should impede understanding, because understanding the metaphor requires reference to the attributive category, not simply reference to the literal shark.

Consider assertions that convey ground-irrelevant properties of metaphor topics and vehicles (e.g., *lawyers can be married* versus *sharks can swim*). According to the attribution model, the topic *lawyers* in the *lawyer-shark* metaphor is understood as referring at only one level of abstraction, to the literal referent *lawyers*. Since literal lawyers can be married, and even married lawyers can be ruthless, reading a sentence that conveys this metaphor-irrelevant property about some lawyers' marital state should not interfere with one's understanding of the metaphor. It could even facilitate understanding, because advance knowledge of the topic of a metaphor can be beneficial. The attribution and the comparison models would thus agree on this prediction.

The two models diverge sharply about the effect of irrelevant vehicle information on comprehension. The assertion that *sharks can swim* does not conflict with the idea that sharks are ruthless, but it does refer to the literal shark rather than to the metaphorical one. *Can swim* is a property of the literal shark, not of the metaphorical one: there can be ruthless creatures for whom the property *can swim* is either false or irrelevant. Thus, the assertion about swimming ability should lead readers to interpret the term *sharks* at an inappropriate level of abstraction, and this in turn should hamper identification of the appropriate category referent. This interference should significantly reduce any facilitation that would ordinarily be produced by advance knowledge of the vehicle term.

In contrast, the comparison model assumes that the topic and the vehicle terms are both understood as referring to their conventional, literal referents. Therefore, the introduction of metaphor-irrelevant properties of the vehicle should not have any deleterious effects. Advance knowledge of the vehicle, either with or without additional irrelevant information, should provide a head start on property extraction and comparison. Thus, ground-irrelevant vehicle primes should be just as effective as ground-irrelevant topic primes. Whatever the effects of irrelevant information might be, they should be equivalent for both topics and vehicles.

McGlone and Manfredi (in press) designed a straightforward test of the competing predictions of the two models. Prior to interpreting a metaphor, the experimental participants (the usual suspects, college undergraduates) read the topic or the vehicle concept alone, or one of two types of property attribution sentences: (a) one that ascribed a metaphor-relevant property to either the metaphor topic or vehicle or (b) one that ascribed a metaphor-irrelevant property to either the metaphor topic or vehicle. For example, for the metaphor *some lawyers are sharks*, the topic and vehicle primes were *lawyer* and *shark*, respectively. The ground-relevant primes were *lawyers can be ruthless* and *sharks can be ruthless*, respectively. The ground-irrelevant primes were *lawyers can be married* and *sharks can swim*, respectively.

The time taken to interpret metaphors with no prior information served as the baseline measure. Relative facilitation or interference was assessed by comparing the time taken to interpret a metaphor following one of the six priming conditions with the baseline time. The results are shown in Figure 4.1. All of the priming conditions except one facilitated comprehension, speeding up interpretation time by about 150 to 250 milliseconds. The exception, as predicted by the dual reference attribution model, was the ground-irrelevant vehicle property, *sharks can swim*. This kind of information actually slowed down comprehension time by over 100 milliseconds, presumably because it drew attention to the literal referent, real sharks, instead of to the more abstract category of predatory creatures that sharks exemplify.

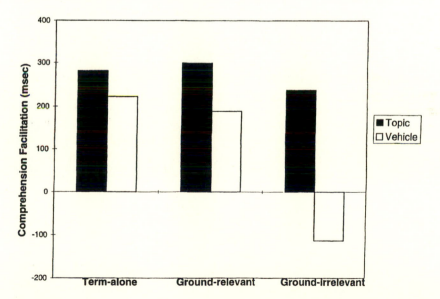

Figure 4.1. Facilitating and interfering with metaphor comprehension as a function of prime type.

These findings are consistent with the notion that metaphor vehicle terms such as *shark* can refer at two different levels of abstraction, with the more general abstract level being the appropriate level for metaphorical interpretation. One implication of this idea is that when one understands a metaphor, one does not consider the literal referent of the metaphor vehicle at all. That is, when one interprets an expression such as *my lawyer was a shark*, one does not include the concept of the literal marine creature, along with its literal properties such as "can swim," in the final interpretation of the metaphor. If it were, then one would be misled to believe that my lawyer can swim, but such irrelevant and inappropriate information should not be part of one's understanding of the original metaphoric expression.

If the metaphor term *shark* does indeed refer uniquely to a general category of predatory beings and not to the marine creature, then metaphor-irrelevant properties of the literal shark, such as "can swim," should not be part of the metaphor interpretation. To assess this prediction of the dual-reference hypothesis, Gernsbacher, Keysar, and Robertson (1995) asked participants to read sentences, one at a time, and to decide whether each statement made sense. Embedded in the list of sentences were metaphors such as *my lawyer is a shark* and literal counterpart sentences such as *the hammerhead is a shark*. The metaphors and the literal sentences served as primes for metaphor-relevant and metaphor-irrelevant probe sentences such as *sharks are vicious* and *sharks are good swimmers*, respectively. The time to judge whether each type of probe was sensible served as a measure of property accessibility. As expected, participants responded more quickly to metaphor-relevant probe sentences after reading metaphors than after reading literal control sentences, suggesting that metaphor-relevant properties become salient during metaphor comprehension. Also as expected, they responded more slowly to metaphor-irrelevant probe sentences after reading metaphors than after reading literal sentences.[9] We replicated these findings not only with a group of college students but with a sample of elderly people age 70 and older. Reassuringly, both the younger and the older people showed the same pattern of results: irrelevant literal information was effectively filtered out during metaphor comprehension (Glucksberg, Newsome & Goldvarg, 1997; see also Galinsky & Glucksberg, 2000).

Dual Reference in Predicative Metaphors

The dual-reference function of metaphor vehicles in nominal metaphors has its analog in predicative metaphors, where verbs are used metaphorically. For example, in expressions such as *the car flew across the intersection* and *the idea flew across town*, the verb *flew* refers to the general action category of fast, direct movement, not to the more specific action of traveling through the air. When we interpret expressions involving flying cars or ideas, the property of being airborne should not be part of our understanding. Just as we should not believe that shark-lawyers can swim, so should we not believe that cars are airborne when they fly through intersections.

If verbs such as *to fly* can be used to refer at two different levels of abstraction—one literal and the other metaphorical—then understanding such verbs in different contexts should lead to different interpretations. In metaphoric contexts, the property of being airborne should not be part of one's interpretation, but in literal contexts this property should be included. Lisa Torreano (1997) adapted Gernsbacher et al's experimental paradigm to see whether verbs have dual reference in the same way that nouns do.

Torreano had people read sentences such as *flying is a fast way to travel* or *flying is travelling in the air*. The use of *fly* in the first sentence is metaphorical and does not necessarily entail being airborne; the use in the second is literal and does entail being airborne. Each of these two types of property sentences—metaphorical and literal—can follow either a metaphor, such as *the idea flew across town*, or a literal expression, such as *the bird flew across town*. The time to judge whether each type of property statement was sensible provided a measure of property accessibility. Just as in the noun-metaphor case, Torreano's subjects responded more quickly to metaphor-relevant property sentences after reading metaphors than after reading literal sentences, indicating that metaphor-relevant information becomes salient during metaphor comprehension. More interesting, the subjects responded more slowly to metaphor-irrelevant literal property sentences after reading metaphors than after reading literal sentences, indicating that such literal properties are effectively filtered out. Verbs, when used metaphorically, refer to the general action category, not to the specific one. The reverse is true when verbs are used literally. Dual reference thus seems operative with verbs as it is with nouns.

In this chapter, we have contrasted the interactive attribution model of metaphor comprehension with the general class of comparison models. Two specific aspects of the attribution model were examined: the differential roles of metaphor topics and vehicles and the dual reference function of metaphor vehicles. In chapter 5, we examine a different type of figurative expression, idioms. Although idioms are usually considered quite different from metaphors—the former always frozen and conventional, the latter often novel and fresh—we argue that they may not be that different after all. As we shall see, some types of idioms behave exactly like metaphors, while others behave exactly like literal language.

Idioms

From Metaphors to "Just Long Words"?

If natural language had been designed by a logician, idioms would not
exist.

Philip Johnson-Laird, 1993

Idioms are a subset of the fixed expressions in a language community.
Jackendoff (1995) estimates that there are as many fixed expressions as
there are words in American English, roughly 80,000. This means that
people have at least 160,000 items memorized and available for use (see
Weinrich, 1966). Jackendoff based his estimate on a corpus drawn from
the television show *Wheel of Fortune,* a game show in which people guess
words and phrases on the basis of minimal cues. Fixed expressions include,
in order of relative frequency, compounds (e.g., frequent flyer program),
idioms (e.g., sitting pretty), names (e.g., Count Dracula, John Deere trac-
tor), clichés (e.g., no money down), song, book, and movie titles (e.g., "All
You Need Is Love"), quotes (e.g., "Beam me up, Scotty"), and familiar
foreign phrases (e.g., au contraire). For Jackendoff, these multiword
phrasal expressions are as much a part of the mental lexicon as are single
words. But, as we shall soon see, phrasal expressions behave quite differently from single words.

What sets idioms apart from most other fixed expressions is their "non-
logical" nature, that is, the absence of any discernable relation between
their linguistic meanings and their idiomatic meanings. Indeed, this characteristic of many (but not all) idioms motivates the usual definition of an
idiom: a construction whose meaning cannot be derived from the meanings
of its constituents. For example, a syntactic and semantic analysis of an
idiom such as *kick the bucket* would never produce the meaning *to die.*

Examples such as *kick the bucket* have led to the deceptively simple view
that idioms are simply memorized expressions, nothing more than long

words, and so require no further analysis or explanation (see Swinney & Cutler, 1979). To learn an idiom, simply memorize its stipulated meaning, and that's that. When a familiar idiom is heard, its meaning is retrieved in the same way that the meaning of a familiar word is retrieved. When a meaning must be expressed for which a familiar idiom is appropriate, then that idiom would be retrieved from memory and produced just as a familiar word would be.

But idioms are not simply long words. They consist of phrases and, more important, behave as do phrases, albeit with certain constraints. Some idioms are syntactically flexible, appearing, for example, in both active and passive forms (e.g., "Who let the cat out of the bag? It was let out by old George, of course.") This example demonstrates yet another characteristic of some idioms. A constituent, in this case the cat, can be referred to anaphorically by the pronoun *it*. If the idiom were simply a long word whose constituents had no meanings of their own, then the idiom should not be syntactically flexible, and one should not be able to replace one of its constituents with a pronoun. Some idioms can also be modified internally, as in *he kicked the proverbial bucket*, or *he didn't spill a single bean*. Again, if these idioms were simply long words, then they should not be capable of such modifications.

These examples illustrate two major issues for a theory of idiom comprehension and use. The first issue concerns compositionality. To what extent are idioms compositional, that is, to what extent can the meaning of an idiom be derived from the meanings of its constituents? As we shall see, degree of compositionality varies greatly among idioms, with some idioms being fully compositional and others not at all. The second issue concerns the syntactic properties of idioms. To what extent does an idiom's meaning depend on its syntactic form, and to what extent can an idiom be open to syntactic analysis and transformation? This issue of syntactic flexibility, like that of compositionality, relates directly to the standard definition of idioms as non logical. If an idiom's constituents have no meaning at all, then the idiom should be incapable of syntactic flexibility. However, idioms can vary from being fully syntactically flexible to not at all. An example of an almost fully flexible idiom is *don't give up the ship*. All of the following variants can be interpreted and would be acceptable in appropriate contexts:

Tense: He will give up the ship; He gave up the ship.
Passivization: The ship was given up by the city council.
Number: Cowardly? You won't believe it: They gave up all the ships!
Adverbial modification: He reluctantly gave up the ship.
Adverbial and adjectival modification: After holding out as long as possible, he finally gave up the last ship.
Word substitution: Give up the ship? Hell, he gave up the whole fleet!

This idiom's flexibility, however, is not completely unconstrained. Some lexical substitutions won't work; for example, the expression *He gave up the boat* is distinctly odd, and most people would view it as a speaker's mistake or perhaps not even recognize the idiom. Similarly, *boot the pail* would not be acceptable and might not even be recognized as a form of *kick the bucket*. The principles that govern the ways in which idioms can be varied lexically or syntactically have yet to be formalized. We return to this issue after a consideration of how idioms are recognized and understood.

Idiom Recognition

People should be able to recognize idioms in the same way that they recognize familiar fixed expressions in general. Indeed, they should recognize idioms and other fixed expressions much as they recognize single words. According to one influential theory of word recognition (Marslen-Wilson, 1987), spoken words are recognized via a process of elimination. Take the case of a word that begins with the syllable "FAH" as in *fodder*. As soon as one hears this syllable, the cohort of words that begin with that syllable becomes available as potential candidates. This cohort includes all the words that are reasonably frequent and familiar, including such words as *foxtrot, foppish, fob, fog, foggy, follow, fop, fond, fondle, fondue, font, fontanel, fossil, fossilize, foster*, and *fought*. If the syllable continues with the sound "x" as in *fox*, then the hearer narrows down the cohort to include only those words that begin with that sequence of sounds. If the word ends at this point, then the word is "fox." Whether it is taken to refer to the animal or to a person who is fox-like, or whether it is a noun or a verb, is determined by the context of the conversation.

Fixed expressions that consist of more than one word can be recognized in much the same way. Fixed expressions, like words, vary in their predictability. Some words, such as *zeitgeist*, begin in a relatively uncommon way,[1] so their identity can be predicted quite early in the recognition process. Others, such as *fodder*, share their initial sound sequences with many other words, and so cannot be identified until later in the process. Similarly, if an expression begins in a unique way, then it can be recognized almost immediately. If, however, the first few words are not unique to that expression, then it cannot be recognized until the alternatives in its cohort can be ruled out. Expressions such as *ballpoint pen* can be recognized before the final word (in this case, *pen*) is uttered. After all, how many expressions beginning with *ballpoint* continue with any word other than *pen*? In contrast, expressions that begin with the word *just* are quite frequent, so such expressions cannot be predicted: it might be any one of a very large number, including those that continue with the words *you wait, around the corner, when you thought it was safe, say no, a minute, a hop skip and a jump, as clear as day, like taking candy from a baby*, and so on.

Idioms, as with other fixed expressions, thus vary in their predictability. An idiom such as *yummy yummy yummy* (cited in Jackendoff, 1995) can be recognized as soon as the second *yummy* begins. In contrast, the idiom *hit the nail on the head* cannot be recognized with any certainty as an idiom until the word *head* occurs. Until that point, or "key word," the phrase might well be intended literally (and even then might be interpreted literally, depending on the context). Tabossi and Zardon (1993, 1995; see also Cacciari & Tabossi, 1988) classified idioms as having either early or late key words. Without a context that could bias interpretation toward idiomatic meaning, idioms with early key words should be recognized faster as idioms than those with late key words. Tabossi and Zardon used a lexical decision task to assess this hypothesis. In their experiment, people listened to idioms with either early or late key words and simultaneously watched a computer screen for the appearance of letter strings. The task was to decide, as quickly as possible, whether each letter string was a word. Examples of an early and a late key-word idiom are:

> Early: Finally Silvio had succeeded in *setting his mind at rest* (resigned).
> Late: In the end, the man *hit the nail on the head* (accurate).

The key word in each of these idioms is italicized, and the words in parentheses are the target words for lexical decision. These target words can appear in one of three positions: just after the sentence verb, or just after either the first or the second content word of the idiom. In Tabossi and Zardon's experiment, the time to make a lexical decision when the target appeared just after the verb (but before the idiom) served as a baseline measure. If an idiomatic meaning had been activated, then it should facilitate recognizing words that are related to that meaning, so lexical decisions to the targets should be faster than baseline. As expected, lexical decision times for target words after the first content word in early-key idioms were faster than baseline, but not those for late-key idioms. For late-key idioms, idiomatic meanings were not activated until after the second content word (e.g., *head* in *hit the nail on the head*). Tabossi and Zardon interpreted this finding to mean that idioms are memorized configurations of words and are recognized when the configuration becomes unique to the idiom.

In this respect, recognizing an idiom is analogous to recognizing a word, but there is a critical difference between word and idiom recognition. When people recognize spoken words, the entire cohort of possible words is activated immediately, and this cohort is continuously narrowed down as more information accumulates. Recognition of a word thus takes place incrementally over time, and the activation of its potential meanings begins very early in the process (McClelland & Elman, 1986; Marslen-Wilson, 1987). In contrast, recognition of an idiom does not seem to proceed incrementally, that is, gradually over time. There is no evidence of any idiomatic meaning activation at all until the key word in the configuration is encountered, at which point the idiomatic meaning is fully activated. This implies very strongly that idioms are not, after all, just long words. They behave like what they are, phrases or configurations of words. And, like literal phrases, idiomatic phrase interpretation seems to be all or none: tentative interpretations are not made until there is enough evidence to support a plausible interpretation (Frazier, 1987). In this respect, idioms are recognized the same way as are literally intended phrasal expressions— segment by segment, and not word by word. Are idioms also understood just as are literal expressions?

Theories of Idiom Comprehension: One Size Fits All?

If idioms formed a unitary class of expressions, then a single theory of idiom comprehension might be possible. A moment's reflection should disabuse one of the hope for a unitary theory of idiom comprehension. Consider two extreme examples, *by and large* and *skating on thin ice*. The former is as close to a long word as a phrase can get in that it behaves pretty much as a long word would behave. Its meaning is arbitrary: it is stipulated to mean "generally." Its meaning is thus noncompositional, that is, its meaning cannot be generated from the syntax and semantics of the idiom's constituents. Syntactic flexibility in such cases is virtually nil: there is no plausible way to transform the idiom into any other syntactic or sequential form. The only exception to these generalizations might be negation, as in the following interchange:

Speaker A: By and large, people are much better off now than they were five years ago.

Speaker B: By and not-so-large. Have you seen the latest figures on poverty and unemployment in urban areas?

Idioms such as *by and large*, then, represent one end of a continuum. Such idioms are syntactically nonanalyzable and semantically noncompositional. Their meanings cannot be inferred from the meanings of their constituent parts, so they are semantically opaque. To all extents and purposes, they are very much like long words, whose meanings are assigned arbitrarily.

At the other end of the continuum are idioms such as *skating on thin ice*, which behave very much like metaphors. Like metaphors, they literally refer to situations, actions, or events that epitomize a class of situations, actions, or events. Skating on thin ice is a prototypical risky action, and so the phrase *skating on thin ice* can be used to refer to any activity that is as risky as that activity. The idiom thus can serve as the name for any such activities, e.g., "trying to develop a unified theory of idioms is skating on thin ice" (especially for young scholars without tenure). And, like nominal metaphors, such idioms can be used either in the class-inclusion or the simile form (e.g., "trying to develop a unified theory of idioms is *like* skating on thin ice.")

Because the literal meanings of such idioms are intimately related to their idiomatic meanings, such idioms behave like comparable literal expressions. They are syntactically analyzable and so can undergo syntactic variation (e.g., "He decided not to skate on thin ice and took the more secure job instead"). Semantic variations that make sense (e.g., "George take risks? Not him, he'll only skate on solid ice") are also permissible. In short, there seems to be no functional difference between these quasi-metaphorical idioms and metaphors. They are fully analyzable syntactically and fully compositional semantically, and their meaning is transparent, that is, if one knows the literal referent, then one can derive the idiomatic meaning.[2] In between are idioms that vary considerably in terms of transparency, syntactic analyzability, and semantic compositionality.

Toward a Functional Classification of Idiom Types

How many kinds of idioms are there, and are they all learned, used, and understood in the same or in different ways? Cacciari and Glucksberg (1991) and Glucksberg (1993), following Nunberg (1978) and Gibbs and Nayak (1989), Gibbs, Nayak, and Cutting (1989), and Gibbs, Nayak, Bolton and Keppel (1989), proposed a functional typology of idioms that is based on their degree of compositionality and semantic transparency. We begin with the assumption that idioms, like other occurrences of natural language, are automatically processed lexically, semantically, and syntactically.[3] Thus, the linguistic meanings of an idiom's constituents are available to contribute to an idiom's meaning and to an idiom's syntactic and semantic flexibility. Whether linguistic meanings have any effects on such flexibility, of course, depends on the idiom type.

As a first cut, idioms can be classified on the dimension of compositionality (Nunberg, 1978). In noncompositional idioms, no relations between the idiom's constituents and the idiom's meaning can be discerned, as in the idiom *cheesecake* to refer to pinup art, or *lemon* to refer to a product that is hopelessly flawed and cannot be repaired (hence the idiomatic phrase *lemon law* to refer to legislation that protects consumers against lemons). In partially compositional idioms, some relationships between an idiom's constituents and its idiomatic meaning can be discerned and exploited. Although one could not infer the meaning *to die* from the literal meaning of *kick the bucket*, the idiom's literal meaning does constrain its use and comprehension. For example, the idiom can be used in the past, present, or future tense, as well as with modal auxiliaries, as in *He might kick the bucket*. Semantically, the literal meaning of the verb *to kick* can permit discourse variations such as

Speaker A: Did the old man kick the bucket last night?
Speaker B: Nah, he barely nudged it.

In fully compositional idioms, the constituents map directly onto their idiomatic referents, as in the idiom *pop the question*. In this idiom, the verb *pop* and the noun phrase *the question* map directly onto the idiomatic meanings of *suddenly utter* and *marriage proposal*. In noncompositional idioms such as *spic and span*, none of the constituents map onto the idiomatic meaning of *neat, clean, and orderly*.

Gibbs and his colleagues conducted an extensive series of studies to determine (a) whether people could reliably classify idioms as either compositional or not and (b) whether compositional idioms are easier to understand than noncompositional ones. For compositional idioms, the results of linguistic analysis would be consistent with the idiomatic meaning, so comprehension should be facilitated. For noncompositional idioms, idiomatic and linguistic meanings would conflict, so comprehension should be more difficult. The evidence is consistent with this initial classification. People have no trouble judging which idioms are compositional and which are not (Gibbs & Nayak, 1989). Also as expected, compositional idioms are understood more quickly than are noncompositional ones (Gibbs, Nayak, & Cutting, 1989).

Idioms can also be classified on the dimension of transparency, that is, the extent to which an idiom's meaning can be inferred from the meanings of its constituents. Given that an idiom is compositional, it may still be either opaque or transparent. In compositional-opaque idioms, the relations between an idiom's constituents and its meaning may be opaque, but the meanings of individual words can nevertheless constrain both interpretation and use. For the idiom *kick the bucket*, the semantics of the verb *to kick* can constrain interpretation. Kicking is a discrete act, and so one could not say *he kicked the bucket all week*, even though one could say *he lay dying all week*. Similarly, kicking is a swift action; when someone *kicks the bucket*, he dies swiftly, as opposed to *giving up the ghost*, which implies going gently into that good night (Glucksberg, 1993; Hamblin & Gibbs, 1999).

Another idiom type is both compositional and transparent. In these idioms, there are one-to-one semantic relations between the idiom's constituents and components of the idiom's meaning. In the idiom *break the ice*, for example, the word *break* corresponds to the idiomatic sense of abruptly changing an uncomfortable social situation, and the word *ice* corresponds to the idiomatic sense of social or interpersonal tension. Similarly, the constituents of the idiom *spill the beans* map directly onto the components of the idiom's meaning. *Spill* refers to the act of revealing and *beans* to heretofore secret information. In this kind of idiom, the meanings might well have been originally opaque. Before learning the idiom's meaning, people would most likely not have been able to infer that *spill the beans* means *reveal the secret*. After learning this idiom's meaning, the words *spill* and *beans* might well acquire their idiomatic meanings as secondary, literal senses.[4] That this can easily occur is suggested by an observation of a three-year-old girl who had been told by her mother that *spilling the beans* meant *disclosing a secret*. Later that day, she told her father, "Don't throw the beans to Rebecca, she's not supposed to know!" (Greenberg-Concool, 1990). Such examples illustrate the very fine line that can exist between the literal and the idiomatic meanings of fixed expressions.

A fourth type of idiom, the quasi-metaphorical, has already been mentioned. These idioms convey meaning via their allusional content. They call to mind a prototypical or stereotypical instance of an entire category of people, events, situations, or actions. These idioms exploit the same communicative strategy as do the metaphor vehicles in nominal metaphors such as *my lawyer was a shark* or *my job is a jail*. In these expressions, vehicles such as *shark* and *jail* allude to ideal exemplars of their metaphorical attributive categories—cutthroat predators and confining situations, respectively—and simultaneously serve as names for those categories (Brown, 1958b; Glucksberg & Keysar, 1990; Glucksberg, McGlone, & Manfredi, 1997). Such metaphors characterize their topics by assigning them to categories that are diagnostic and often evaluative, as in *Kenneth Starr is a bulldozer*. Quasi-metaphorical idioms function precisely the same as nominal metaphors. Via the mechanism of dual reference, they can simultaneously refer to an ideal exemplar of a concept and characterize some event or situation as an instance of that concept. For the concept *doing something prematurely*, for example, one might use the metaphorical idiom *crossing one's bridges before coming to them*.

Speaker A: Shouldn't we prepare now for the possibility of Clinton's impeachment?
Speaker B: We'll cross that bridge when we come to it.

In this interchange, B identifies premature concern by using the idiom about crossing bridges. This places the two actions in a common category. Doing something prematurely and crossing a bridge before getting to it are analogues of each other, and both are instances of the category of actions that are performed before their time. Premature action, in turn, is referred to by the allusion to an ideal exemplar of such an action, crossing a bridge before coming to it. Because such idioms are fully compositional, they can be varied and still make sense. If, for example, the future situation seems totally hopeless, speaker B could well have said, "We'll jump off that bridge when we come to it." Similarly, the metaphorical idiom *he burned his bridges behind him* can be expressed as *he burned all of his bridges in front of him* to refer to a person engaged in self-destructive behavior.

We have now identified four types of idioms: noncompositional (e.g., *by and large*), which by definition are not transparent; compositional opaque (e.g., *kick the bucket*); compositional transparent (e.g., *spill the beans*); and quasi-metaphorical (e.g., *skating on thin ice*). Other scholars have proposed somewhat different typologies, for example, Nunberg (1978) with fewer types and Gibbs and Nayak (1989) with more, but there is agreement on the importance of compositionality and transparency. Given the typology offered here, how do the various theories of idiom comprehension account for each idiom type?

How Are Idioms Understood? Let Me Count the Ways

Early theories of idiom comprehension took, as a starting point, the traditional pragmatic model of figurative language understanding. As with such models of metaphor comprehension, literal priority was assumed. An idiomatic meaning would be sought if and only if a linguistic analysis failed. This class of models can be ruled out summarily by the troublesome fact that idioms are understood as quickly as comparable literal expressions (Ortony, Schallert, Reynolds, & Antos, 1978; Gibbs, 1980; Tabossi & Cacciari, 1988). Indeed, highly familiar idioms, such as *spill the beans* and *kick the bucket*, are understood more quickly in their idiomatic sense than in their literal sense (Gibbs, 1980; McGlone, Glucksberg, & Cacciari, 1994).

Early theories also took as a given that (all?) idioms are noncompositional. Bobrow & Bell (1973) proposed the idiom-list hypothesis. Idioms were considered to be fixed expressions whose meanings were listed in a special idiom module. When one encounters an idiom and a literal reading of it makes no sense, then one seeks a meaning from the idiom list. The literal-priority aspect of the theory is obviously wrong. It is even undermined by Bobrow and Bell's own finding that when people expect idioms, then they can get into an idiom mode and understand idioms faster than when they do not know what kinds of expressions to expect. The notion that idioms are noncompositional, with meanings that must be retrieved from memory, cannot be ruled out entirely, but this aspect of the theory is at once more limited and more general than originally intended. It is more limited because it applies to only a small subset of idioms, those that are noncompositional and opaque. It is also more general in that it is applicable not only to such idioms but also to all other fixed expressions that are noncompositional and opaque. These include, among others, proper names (e.g., Ali Baba), place names (e.g., Oklahoma), brand names (e.g., Hostess Twinkies), exclamations (e.g., son of a gun), and foreign-language phrases (e.g., terra firma; see Jackendoff, 1995). There seems to be no convincing motivation to postulate separate memory stores for different kinds of noncompositional, opaque fixed expressions, so we can expand Bobrow and Bell's notion of an idiom list to include all such expressions, namely something like Jackendoff's phrasal lexicon.

Another early theory of idiom comprehension has already been mentioned in connection with how idioms are recognized. The notion that idioms are nothing other than long words was made explicit by Swinney and Cutler (1979) in their lexicalization hypothesis. This hypothesis accounts very nicely for the relative ease of with which people understand familiar idioms. When an idiom is encountered, two sets of operations begin in parallel: ordinary linguistic processing, including lexical access and syntactic parsing, and, simultaneously, retrieval from the phrasal lexicon where idioms-as-long-words are stored. Which of the two meanings—literal or idiomatic—appears first depends on the relative speed with which linguistic processing and lexical-idiom access can be completed. Normally, idiom access is completed more quickly because it does not require the lexical, syntactic, and semantic processing involved in full linguistic analysis. Thus, familiar idioms are generally understood more quickly than are comparable literal expressions.

Gibbs (1984) proposed a more extreme version of the direct idiom-access model. Rather than positing a race between idiom meaning retrieval and linguistic processing, Gibbs argued that people do not engage in any linguistic analysis of familiar idioms at all and so can bypass literal meanings entirely. Again, the primary evidence for this position is the relative speed of idiom comprehension. The evidence against this view includes the automaticity of language processing (Stroop, 1935; Miller & Johnson-Laird, 1976) and the syntactic and semantic flexibility of idiom use. If idioms such as *kick the bucket* can accept syntactic and anaphoric operations, then they must, perforce, have been analyzed linguistically. Perhaps the most compelling evidence against direct access without any linguistic processing stems from the way that people understand idiom variants, that is, idioms in noncanonical form.

Idiom Variants and Linguistic Processing

If idioms are simply long words, then it should be quite difficult to understand idioms when they appear in novel formats. How do people manage to understand expressions such as *He didn't spill a single bean*? The meaning of this variant expression cannot be stored in memory because the expression is novel, albeit based on a familiar idiom. Because a variant's meaning is not directly available in memory, the meanings of the constituents must be accessed and used in some fashion to derive the idiom's meaning. There are two possibilities explanations. The first is compatible with direct-access models, including those proposed by Swinney and Cutler and by Gibbs. When one encounters a variant idiom, one must first recognize it as a variant of a familiar idiom. Once this is done, one then compares the meanings of the original and the variant idiom constituents. One ascertains the relationships between the constituent meanings and, by analogy, infers the meaning of the variant. This strategy involves, at minimum, the following six steps:

1. Recognize the idiom as a variant of a conventional idiom.
2. Retrieve the meaning of the original idiom.
3. Identify the constituent meanings of both the variant and the original idioms.
4. Compare the constituent meanings of the two idiom forms.
5. Identify the relation(s) between those meanings (e.g., verb tense, quantification, negation).
6. On the basis of this relation, infer the relation between the meanings of the original and variant idioms.

If, for example, a substituted word is an antonym of a word in the original, then the variant's meaning could be taken as the opposite of the original, as in *got up on the right side of the bed* instead of *got up on the wrong side of the bed*. If the relation between the substituted words is one of quantity, then this could be taken as the relation between the idiom meanings, as in *spill a single bean* versus *spill the beans*. More complex relationships are also possible, as in the example provided in a *New York Times* article on the rise and fall of a Wall Street brokerage firm, Drexel Burnham Lambert. Drexel and company had flourished by peddling junk bonds but then found itself with a serious cash flow problem. The firm considered declaring bankruptcy, but before doing so it distributed the firm's assets among the senior executives in the form of substantial cash bonuses. This forced the firm into bankruptcy, prompting the *Times* reporter to coin this twist on a familiar idiom: "Drexel's senior executives, not content with collecting one golden egg after another, seem to have insisted then on eating the goose." Similarly, Donald Barthelme's title for an essay on contemporary literature, "Convicted Minimalist Spills Bean," makes perfect sense to those who know of his reputation as a minimalist writer.

Intuitively, we seem to understand these twists on old idioms quite easily, without any conscious awareness of laboriously comparing meanings between the novel and the original idiom forms. We certainly do not seem to need any more time to understand novel twists than to understand ordinary language. However, the six-step model outlined earlier implies that understanding novel idiom variants should be quite difficult. On the six-step model, original idioms should be understood quite quickly because they require only memory retrieval. Linguistic processing undoubtedly occurs (cf. Cacciari & Tabossi, 1988; Tabossi & Zardon, 1995) but need not be used to arrive at the idiom's meaning. In contrast, idiom twists should take longer not only than their originals but also than comparable literal expressions. The reason for this is that the twists require more operations than comparable literal expressions; one must not only derive literal meanings but also compare the meanings of the original's and the variant's constituents, as well as the relation between the original and the variant idiomatic meanings.

An alternative strategy is much simpler. In general, idioms that permit sensible variants tend to be compositional and transparent; the relations between the idiom's constituents and its meanings tend to be systematic, as in *spill the beans*. With such idioms, the constituents often become polysemous through frequent use in idiom contexts. Thus, the verb and the noun in the idiom *spill the beans* have at least two senses: their default context-free literal meanings and the meanings that are appropriate in the idiom context. In nonidiomatic contexts, the verb *spill* usually has the meaning *to be lost from a container* and the word *beans* the meaning *edible legumes*. In the idiom context, these words have a dual meaning; they retain their literal meanings but also have the idiomatic meanings of *reveal* and *secrets*.

Once this property of polysemy has developed for a particular idiom and its constituents, variants of the original idiom can be processed just as one would process any other phrase or sentence: by accessing the contextually appropriate word meanings and performing ordinary linguistic analyses of the words and their grammatical relations. For familiar idioms, this results in at least two products: the literal meaning and the idiomatic meaning, including the idiomatic senses of the idiom constituents.

This model has two interesting advantages over the standard idiom direct-access model. First, it allows for rapid and easy comprehension and production of variant idioms.[5] Second, it is parsimonious. The same model accounts for comprehension of idioms in both their canonical and their variant forms. According to this model, variant idioms should take longer to understand in their variant than in their canonical forms because the variants must undergo linguistic analysis, which presumably takes more time than simple retrieval of an idiom's meaning from memory. However, variants should take no longer than comparable literal expressions. The standard model, outlined earlier, predicts that variants will take longer than both original idioms and comparable literal expressions.

To test these predictions, McGlone, Glucksberg, and Cacciari (1994) compared comprehension times for original and variant idioms and their literal paraphrases. They presented short vignettes on a computer screen, one line at a time, which the experimental participants read at their own pace, pressing a key to advance the text line by line. The target expressions were embedded in appropriate contexts, as in this example:

> Lieutenant Sam Murphy was a pilot during the war. While conducting a reconnaissance mission, he was shot down over enemy territory and captured. When he was presented before one of the enemy commanders, Sam was interrogated for details of an attack that his squadron was rumored to be plotting. He knew the entire battle plan but didn't let on that he was aware of any scheme. The commander quickly grew tired of his prisoner's reluctance to cooperate. After torturing him for three hours to no avail, the commander threatened to kill him if the plans weren't disclosed. *Sam spilled the beans/Sam told him all/Sam didn't spill a single bean/Sam didn't say a single word.* Sam felt his life/honor was much more important than honor/his life.

As expected, idioms in canonical form were read more quickly than either their variants or their literal paraphrases. This is consistent with both hypotheses. Idiom meanings can often be retrieved from memory before linguistic processing can be completed. More interesting, the idiom variants were read just as quickly as their literal counterparts; that is, *didn't spill a single bean* was read as quickly as *didn't say a single word.* This is consistent with the notion that variant idioms, like literal expressions, require linguistic processing, but no additional processing beyond that. Comparable data and conclusions were reported by Van de Voort and Vonk (1995) in a study that used Dutch idioms. The bottom line is that many familiar idioms are compositional, as evidenced by the fact that they can be modified syntactically and semantically and still be easily understood.

Compositionality Reconsidered

Although I have used idiom modification as evidence for the compositionality of various idiom types, Nicolas (1995) takes a diametrically opposed view. Like Davidson (1977), who argued that metaphors "have no meaning," Nicolas argues that "none of the individual words in an idiom, but only the idiom as a whole, has meaning" (p. 235). When an idiom is internally modified, as in *call the political tune*, Nicolas claims that the word *tune* is not the object of the modifier *political*, but rather the entire idiom. If an internal adjectival modification can be paraphrased as an adverbial (e.g., *dominate politically speaking*), then there is no need to assume that the individual word *tune* has meaning in the context of the idiom. Some of his other examples include: pull *no* strings → *not* exert influence and beat about the *proverbial* bush → beat about the bush *as the saying goes*.[6]

While it may be the case that the component parts of idioms do not carry meaning within a particular linguistic theory or grammar, people's understanding and use of idiomatic expressions clearly show evidence of constituent meanings, that is, the literal meanings of idiom constituents often play important roles in comprehension and use. Occasionally, such meanings can play mischievous roles, as when idioms are gotten not quite right by second-language learners.

Philip Roth's character Drenka, in his novel *Sabbath's Theater* (1994), provides some fictional but all too representative examples. Drenka is an immigrant woman from Croatia who has spent thirteen years in the United States. She has become "syntactically urbane." Believing herself to be "smoothly idiomatic," she produces unforgettable utterances by which people remember her, even after her death. Some of her creations are "bear and grin it," "you are pulling my leg out," "an early bird is never late," "you can't teach an old dog to sit," and "it takes two to tangle" (Roth, 1995, pp. 72–73). For native speakers, such distortions are rare, but they do occasionally occur. During a discussion of the difficulties of obtaining federal research funding, one of my colleagues observed that "new grants are as scarce as pig's teeth." It was only after I had pointed out that pigs have lots of teeth that he and others in the conversation became aware of his substitution of "pig" for "hen." Obviously, the literal meanings of "hen" and "pig" as farm animals played a role in this slip of the tongue. In this case, literal meanings played a nonfunctional role. What determines how and when such literal meanings play functional roles in idiom comprehension and use?

Idiom Productivity: A Discourse-Based Perspective

In general, idioms that are compositional and transparent tend to be syntactically and lexically flexible (Gibbs, Nayak, & Cutting, 1989). Compositionality, however, is neither a necessary nor a sufficient condition for an idiom to be varied productively. Consider idioms whose constituents cannot be mapped individually onto their idiomatic meaning(s). One such idiom type uses single-argument predicates, such as *two left feet* to describe clumsiness. The noun phrase *two left feet* consists of three constituent words, and these three words cannot be mapped individually onto the idiomatic referent *clumsy*. Nevertheless, such idioms can still be used productively because the semantics of the phrase as a whole can have direct functional relations with the idiom's stipulated meaning. Variations of an idiom can be productive whenever the variation plausibly exploits such relations. The expression *two left feet*, for example, alludes to the clumsy way someone might dance if he did, indeed, have two left feet. By analogy, number of left feet can be mapped onto different degrees of clumsiness: One left foot would be normal, while three left feet would imply Really clumsy!

This example suggests a general principle that governs productive idiom flexibility. When one or more of an idiom's constituents bears a functional relation to the idiom's meaning, then operations such as tense marking, quantification, antonymy, and negation (among others) can be productive, provided that a plausible communicative intent can be inferred (Cacciari & Glucksberg, 1991; Glucksberg, 1993; Van de Voort & Vonk, 1995). The change from plural to singular in Donald Barthelme's essay title "Convicted Minimalist Spills Bean," for example, is productive because of the transparent relation between the singular *bean* and the concept of minimalism. In contrast, the phrase *popped the questions* would be difficult to interpret because people normally do not propose marriage to more than one person at a time. Thus, even though *questions* is well formed syntactically and semantically, it makes no sense in the context of the idiom. The constraints of world knowledge together with the conventions of discourse and conversation are as important for idiom flexibility as are more formal linguistic factors such as compositionality.

Why Spilling the Peas Is Like Kicking the Pail

We are now in a position to speculate about why certain lexical substitutions are productive, while others are not. What kinds of variations and substitutions do speakers and writers use? Let us begin by considering what kinds of variations are rarely, if ever, used (at least not used intentionally). It is difficult to imagine a context in which someone would say *kick the pail* instead of *kick the bucket*, or *spill the peas* instead of *spill the beans*. These two idioms differ sharply in their formal characteristics: *kick the bucket* is compositional and opaque, *spill the beans* is compositional and transparent. Yet both resist synonym substitution of the predicate noun. The most likely reason is that one cannot easily imagine a motivation for such substitutions. What communicative intent might prompt a speaker to choose *pail* over *bucket* or *peas* over *beans*, other than to be cute? Thus, where no communicative intent can be inferred, listeners may either fail to recognize the idiom itself or may recognize it but view the variant utterance as a mistake by the speaker.

The more interesting case, of course, occurs when speakers intentionally create a novel form by using words that bear an interpretable relation to the original idiom, as in *pour the beans* to communicate that someone was divulging secrets quite lavishly. If a listener decides that a speaker's choice of *pour* over *spill* is intentional, then she might interpret the variant idiom as denoting a more vigorous and egregious disclosure of information than is appropriate for the circumstances. If, however, the choice of *pour* is viewed as a slip of the tongue, then no such communicative intent would be inferred. Given that a variant idiom is recognized as such, the variant will be productive if there is an interpretable relation between the original constituents and their substitutes and the variant is viewed as intentional, not inadvertent. In contrast to unmotivated or accidental synonym substitutions, semantically productive operations serve communicative functions. Some relatively simple productive operations include:

1. Adjectival modification, as in "When drugs are involved, it's time to speak your *parental* mind."
2. Adverbial modification, as in "Did he *finally* speak his mind?"
3. Quantification, as in "As a diverse but purposeful group, you should speak your *minds*."
4. Tense marking, as in "He spoke his mind."
5. All of these, as in "The members of the tenants' association finally spoke their respective minds."

This example is noteworthy because this particular idiom is noncompositional in Gibbs, Nayak, and Cutting's (1989) typology and so should be both lexically and syntactically frozen. Yet this idiom is obviously quite flexible and productive.

Semantic productivity can thus be independent of compositionality and transparency. Instead of being governed by the formal characteristics of idiomatic expressions or by idiom type, productivity is governed by the same principles that govern such discourse phenomena as adjectival and adverbial modification, quantification, and negation. For example, one can sing sweetly if one is actually singing music, but one cannot sing sweetly if one is singing to police detectives. In the detective context, singing refers to an act of disclosing information, not to a musical performance. But, even though one cannot sing sweetly to the police, one can still sing like a canary, that is, sing volubly and with unseemly verve and enthusiasm.

Note that there is nothing in the lexical or syntactic form of the idiomatic verb *to sing* that constrains adjectival modification, only the conventional knowledge of what it means to sing to the authorities. Similarly, there is nothing in the lexical or syntactic form of *speak your mind* that constrains any of its variants. What matters are the communicative intentions that can motivate a speaker to employ a variant. This means that syntactic and lexical flexibility may be relatively independent of idiom type.

Do Idiom Types Constrain Idiom Flexibility?

If flexibility is at least partially determined by compositionality, then we can expect compositional idioms to be more flexible than noncompositional ones. However, this does not preclude flexibility in noncompositional idioms, as seen in the *speak your mind* examples. To see how noncompositional idioms might be used flexibly, let us examine the noncompositional idiom *by and large*. This idiom offers little if any lexical flexibility. When synonyms or antonyms are substituted for the original constituents, the idiom may become unrecognizable; people would most likely not even think of the original *by and large* if they encountered *by plus large* or *by and small*. However, even an idiom as noncompositional and opaque as this one can be productively varied, as when someone says *by and not-so-large* to express disagreement with a generalization.

The productive use of negation in this idiom points up the inadequacy of viewing any idiom as a purely noncompositional string. If an idiom is truly noncompositional, then the scope of negation—or, more generally, the scope of modification—must be limited to the entire string. A negation or an adjective cannot be used to modify a semantically empty element or constituent within a string (Cruse, 1986; Schenk, 1995). In some cases, when an idiom constituent is modified, as in *break the proverbial ice*, it can be treated as a metalinguistic comment on the expression as a whole (Nicolas, 1995). Nevertheless, there is an important difference between such metalinguistic comments and true semantic modification, as in the *by and large* example, or as in such cases as *he broke the really frigid ice*, where the concept of social stiffness is intensified, not merely commented upon. Furthermore, using Nicolas's paraphrase test, this adjectival modification cannot be sensibly paraphrased adverbially (although Nicolas might relegate this example to the category of "word play"; see note 6).

Compositional idioms, whether opaque of transparent, are generally more flexible than noncompositional ones, but here too pragmatic considerations are paramount. For opaque idioms such as *kick the bucket*, where the idiom constituents bear no relation to the idiom's meaning, lexical substitutions are comprehensible only if the original idiom is called to mind. Even then, no communicative intent is inferred if there is no interpretable relation between a substituted word and the original. As noted earlier, the substitution of *booted* for *kicked* or *pail* for *bucket* has no clear motivation and so might be understood but viewed as a mistake. However, one could imagine a context in which a lexical substitution would make sense, as in our earlier example, "no, he barely *nudged* it" in response to a question about whether someone had kicked the bucket. In this case there is clear internal constituent modification: substitution of *nudge* for *kick* and anaphoric reference to *bucket* by the pronoun *it*. As we saw with the *by and large* example, an essentially noncompositional, opaque idiom can still be varied productively if there are discernable relations between a modification and an idiom's original meaning and referents.

Syntactic operations upon idioms are also constrained primarily by the semantics and pragmatics of an idiom's constituents. Consider how *kick the bucket* might be varied syntactically. As noted earlier, kicking is a discrete action, and so even though one can lie dying for a week, one cannot say, "he lay kicking the bucket for a week." In contrast, one could say "almost, will, can, might, may, should, or didn't kick the bucket." Semantic constraints are also operative: *he silently and swiftly kicked the bucket* is interpretable because both dying and kicking can be accomplished silently and swiftly. *He sharply kicked the bucket* is not interpretable, because although one can kick sharply, there is no clear way to understand how anyone could die "sharply" (Wasow, Sag, & Nunberg, 1983).

Pragmatic considerations also operate to block the passive voice for this idiom. People generally do not accept *the bucket was kicked by John* as a paraphrase of *John kicked the bucket*. The communicative role of the passive construction provides a good reason for this. Passives are used to place focus on the object of a clause or a sentence, usually when there is prior topicalization, as in *The woman had just turned the corner when she was hit by a truck*. No such communicative purpose can be served by topicalizing *bucket*, so the passive voice is not interpretable. In principle, a syntactic operation on an idiom is acceptable (i.e., interpretable) if and only if a reasonable communicative intention can be inferred. Otherwise, it will be viewed as a mistake or a lame attempt to be clever. For opaque idioms, the passive voice is rarely if ever used because there is seldom a reason to topicalize or focus on a grammatical or logical object. In contrast, tense markings for such idioms should be interpretable provided that those tense markings make sense for the idiomatic meaning itself, that is, whenever the referent of the expression can take place at different times.

Transparent idioms such as *break the ice* and *spill the beans* are governed by the same pragmatic principles that govern opaque idiom use. An important difference is that the constituents of transparent idioms can often be mapped onto the components of the idiom's meaning. When this condition holds, then any operations that obey the following three constraints should be interpretable. First, the semantics of each idiom constituent must be respected. Second, the relationships between the idiom constituents and the components of the idiomatic meaning must be preserved. Third, a plausible communicative intent must be inferable from the relationship between the original and the varied idioms. For example, the following lexical substitutions satisfy the first two conditions: *crack the ice, break the frost*, and *break the chill*. In each of these cases, the concept of discrete breaking is preserved, and the metaphorical relation between the physical temperature and social warmth/coolness is also preserved. However, no clear communicative intent is apparent, and so, while these variants might be understood, the only inferable communicative intent is stylistic. These variants might even be viewed as ill-formed, unintended mistakes. *Shatter the ice*, on the other hand, is more likely to be viewed as a variant intended to communicate a particularly abrupt change in the social climate. In contrast, *crushed the ice* should be unacceptable because the metaphorical ice of this idiom is not the kind that can be crushed. It is, metaphorically speaking, thin and brittle, capable of being discretely broken but not gradually crushed.

At the syntactic level, the same principles apply. Any syntactic operations that satisfy both the semantics and the pragmatics of an idiom's constituents and the idiom's meaning should be appropriate—again with the important proviso that a communicative intent can be inferred. For example, the passive form works whenever it is appropriate to focus on a grammatical object, as in *the ice was finally broken* or *despite eighteen hours of intensive questioning, not a bean was spilled*.

The insufficiency of compositionality as a determinant of idiom productivity is best illustrated by quasi-metaphorical idioms. These idioms are fully compositional. A literal, linguistic analysis yields a fully adequate interpretation, provided that one is familiar with the cultural or proverbial allusion. The literal meaning of *carrying coals to Newcastle*, for example, is relevant and intended, even though it is insufficient for interpretation. People who use this idiom intend the literal meaning to refer to the action of carrying coal to Newcastle as an ideal exemplar of the general class of situations involving bringing something to a place where it is clearly not needed.[7] Even though this idiom is fully compositional and transparent, lexical substitutions generally do not work. For example, *carrying wood to Birmingham* doesn't make much sense, and even *carrying fuel to Texaco* stretches the limits of recognizability. When, however, a communicative intent can be inferred, then well-chosen paraphrases can be highly effective. A case in point involves a nuclear generating station in Shoreham, Long Island, that had been plagued for years with operating and financial difficulties. A newspaper article on the conversion of the generating station to conventional fuel carried the heading "Carrying Coals to Shoreham." This headline reminded readers of the original idiom, while alluding to the original Shoreham debacle.

The principles that govern syntactic operations upon quasi-metaphorical idioms are also pragmatically based. Syntactic operations must be motivated by a communicative intent, so any changes that they produce in an idiom's meaning must be interpretable in context. The passive voice again provides clear examples. For many quasi-metaphorical idioms, no communicative purpose is served by focusing on the grammatical object.

Thus, it makes no sense to say, *Newcastle was where the coals were carried to*. However, this constraint on passivization is content specific, not a general principle. Some metaphorical idioms make sense in the passive, as in *after years of murderous warfare, the hatchet was finally buried once and for all*. In this case, the grammatical object, *hatchet*, can sensibly be the focus of the expression. The applicability of any syntactic operation is governed by such communicative considerations.

Finally, discourse productivity for quasi-metaphorical idioms is also governed primarily by pragmatic considerations. One can easily imagine a context in which the following interchange would make perfect sense:

Speaker A: Don't worry, I'll cross that bridge when I come to it.
Speaker B: By that time they will have burnt it down!

Here, as in earlier examples, the semantics of an idiom constituent, in this case *bridge*, can be exploited to generate an appropriate conversational response to the original idiom. While retaining its role as a symbol, *bridge* can still be treated as if it were a real bridge so long as its symbolic function is not compromised.

How Idioms Are Learned

Idioms, just like other fixed expressions, must be memorized. Depending on the learner and the idiom type, this process can be trivially easy or maddeningly difficult. Children learning their native language (or languages) seem to pick up idioms quite easily, particularly if they are compositional and transparent. Furthermore, they treat idioms as if they were simply instances of ordinary language. Recall the example of the three-year-old who, upon being told that *spilling the beans* meant revealing secrets, urged her father to keep a secret by saying, "Don't throw the beans to Rebecca, she's not supposed to know." It is exactly this temptation—indeed compulsion—to treat idiom constituents as meaningful that can impede both one's original learning of an expression and one's learning how to use that expression appropriately.[8] For this reason, among others, idioms pose particular problems for people learning a second language.

When people begin learning a second language, they often resort to translating utterances in the new language into their native tongue. This does not pose insurmountable problems for expressions that are intended literally. It also poses no particular difficulties for fixed expressions that cannot be translated but have no literal meanings per se, such as proper names, nonsense strings such as *tra-la-la*, or exclamations such as *ouch!* Such expressions need only to be memorized, and there is no reason to suspect that people learning a second language suffer from either short- or long-term memory problems. Furthermore, such expressions do not rely on culture-specific knowledge.

Problems arise when culture-specific knowledge is involved or when an expression's literal meaning might interfere with understanding. Most idioms, including compositional and transparent ones, cannot survive literal translation. This is especially true of idioms that translation theorists consider oligosemic, that is, those whose meanings are embedded in the culture (Catford, 1965). Consider *go to bat*. If translated literally into French, it might direct the learner to approach a nocturnal animal ("allez au chauve-souris"). Note that *go to bat* is an example of idioms that are both polysemic and oligosemic, rendering access by translation impossible. Similarly, idiomatic newspaper headlines that exploit familiar idioms in one language community would be utterly opaque to people from a different community. How, for example, would a visitor from Spain possibly understand that the newspaper headline "Bulls Shove Chicken Little Aside" refers to a reversal of a financial bear market by alluding to the classic tale of Chicken Little (*New York Times*, September 9, 1998, p. A1; a related idiom twist was "Main Street bulls take bears by the horns").

And, of course, translating an idiom from another language into English can also fail. If the Spanish idiom *no hay Moros en la costa* were to be literally translated, one would come up with "there are no Moors on the shore," a perfectly compositional and transparent expression in a culture that has a history of conflict with peoples from North Africa. However, it is utterly opaque in North American culture, where the analogous idiom is *the coast is clear*. Similarly, the French *casser sa pipe*, whose literal translation is "to break one's pipe," would not translate into *kick the bucket*.

While transparency does not fully solve the problem of idiom learning, it does help. People learning English as a second language often have very limited knowledge of American idioms. However, idioms whose meanings could be inferred from their literal meanings are generally better known by second-language learners than those that are either opaque or oligosemic (Engel, 1996). The influence of culture is apparent in differences in idiom knowledge among different groups of recently arrived immigrants. In a sample of immigrants whom Engel interviewed, those who came from Western American cultures such as Haiti and the Dominican Republic knew substantially more idioms than did people from China, even though both groups had arrived in the United States at about the same time. After all, people from the Dominican Republic have a basis for understanding idioms such as "pinch-hit for," but this idiom would make no sense to people unfamiliar with baseball.[9]

Idioms, in general, are deeply connected to culture. Agar (1991) proposes that biculturalism and bilingualism are two sides of the same coin. Engaged in the intertwined process of culture change, learners have to understand the full meaning of idioms. For Agar, idioms are "rich points." They tap deeply into the world that accompanies language. In his first-person account of achieving understanding of the Austrian idiom *schmah*, meaning "a basic ironic premise that things are not what they seem, and all you can do is laugh it off," Agar argues that to understand *schmah*, one must be steeped in Austrian culture (Agar, 1991, pp. 177–178). Stengel (1939) was perhaps the most articulate in emphasizing the importance of idiomaticity in a new language. He relates it to the discomforts of culture change:

> acquiring a new language in adult life is an anachronism and many people cannot easily tolerate the infantile situation. . . . [I]n some people a feeling of shame arises when they have managed to say something in a foreign language, particularly when saying something specific, e.g., an idiom. Idioms are largely responsible for specific features of language. Idiomatic speech is a kind of secret speech . . . [idioms] are riddles. . . . They are the traps in a language . . . they are petrified jokes and their symbolism is very often incomprehensible. . . . [W]e feel the strange effect of foreign idioms because they force on us . . . pictorial thinking . . . [W]hile learning, we often suspect a latent original idea behind the word. (Stengel, 1939, pp. 476–477)

And, just as learning the idioms of a language community involves acculturation to that community, so do communities and subcommunities develop their own private languages. Jargon, slang, metaphors, and idioms encode important cultural beliefs, norms, and attitudes and serve both as a sign and as a reinforcer of social cohesion. Every community, from the country as a whole to individual families, shares a unique world of expressions. For people such as E. D. Hirsch (1988), all Americans not only should but also must know a minimal set of things if they are to be culturally literate. These "things" all have names and so constitute a list of fixed expressions that, according to Jackendoff (1995), are part of the lexicon. Among the things all Americans should know, are

> Dates: 1066, 1492, and 1984 (Orwell's book title).
> Proper names: Hank Aaron, Chuck Berry, Rene Descartes.
> Proverbs: All that glitters is not gold.
> And, of course, idioms: Albatross around one's neck; at large; cut the Gordian knot; kill with kindness. (Hirsch, 1988)

For a somewhat smaller unit than America as a whole, Microsoft provides a microcosm of what every hacker should know, as embodied in their social vocabulary and idioms. Among the expressions coined and used by Microsoft employees are:

> Blue badge: (Sometimes slightly derogatorily, *blue badger*). Synonym for full-time Microsoft employees, the Brahmins of the deeply ingrained Microsoft caste system, whose card keys have a blue background rather than the orange used for contractors and the green used for vendors. Derivative terms include "turn blue," meaning to earn full-time status.
> Bleeding edge: A variant of the idiom *cutting edge*, with the added implication of a pioneer's vulnerability, as in, "We're really on the bleeding edge with this product. Hope it sells through."
> Eye candy: Visually attractive material, analogous to "ear candy" in the music business and to "arm candy" in the upmarket escort business.

Fiber media: Material published on the archaic medium of paper. Example: "Yeah, I used to be a writer in fiber media, but now I'm a content provider in cybermedia."

Face-mail: Technologically backward means of communication, clearly inferior to voice mail or E-mail. Involves actually walking into someone's office and speaking to him or her face to face. Considered highly inefficient and declassé. (Barnes, 1998)

As many of these examples indicate, attitudes and norms are often inextricably bound up with such idiomatic expressions. People talk not only to communicate propositional content but also to reflect upon and express attitudes and emotions. Idioms, metaphors, and many fixed expressions reflect social norms and beliefs. To learn a culture's idioms and other fixed expressions is to immerse oneself in that culture.

In this and the preceding chapters, we have considered metaphors and idioms in the context of conversation and communication. In important ways, metaphors and idioms reflect both universal and culture-specific ways of thinking. Recent work in cognitive linguistics goes much further, claiming that metaphors and idioms do not simply reflect or communicate ideas but instead constitute ideas and concepts. The most extreme version of this claim argues that people's everyday concepts, such as our concepts of arguments, love, justice, and friendship, are not merely expressed metaphorically but are, at root, metaphorical in nature. We examine this claim in detail in chapter 6.

Concepts as Metaphors

Contributed by Matthew S. McGlone

> Our ordinary conceptual system, in terms of which we both think and
> act, is fundamentally metaphorical in nature.
>
> Lakoff and Johnson, 1980

The phrasal lexicon that people use to describe abstract concepts, such as
idea or time, and emotions, such as love or anger, is replete with metaphoric expressions. Language scholars have long noted that such expressions not only are ubiquitous in the vocabulary we use to describe certain
concepts but also appear to cluster around a limited set of metaphoric
themes (McTaggart, 1908; Bierwisch, 1967; Clark, 1973; Lakoff & Johnson,
1980). For example, consider the thematic similarity among the metaphoric
expressions that are used to describe a love relationship in this fictitious
"break-up" speech:

> Dearest, we've *come a long way* since we first met, but I'm afraid that our
> relationship has finally *hit a dead-end*. It's not *going anywhere*, and we're both
> tired of just *spinning our wheels*. I don't think either of us knows how to *salvage*
> it, so maybe we should just *go our separate ways*.

None of these expressions is particularly poetic, nor is any of them usually
employed to create special rhetorical effects. They are all conventional
phrases that, although not restricted to descriptions of love (e.g., I've
come a long way in this business, but my career has finally *hit a dead
end*), are readily understood when applied to love. The phrases code
different aspects of the love relationship, but they are thematically similar
in that all imply a metaphoric correspondence between love and journeys.
The lovers correspond to travelers, the relationship corresponds to a
traveling vehicle, the lovers' goals correspond to destinations, problems
in the relationship correspond to obstacles in the path of travel, and so

on. Clearly, these metaphoric correspondences offer a linguistically productive strategy for talking about love, as revealed by the numerous conventional expressions that instantiate it and the opportunities for novel extension that they provide (e.g., *we're riding on the freeway of love, wind against our backs*, a line from a classic Aretha Franklin song). What role do these correspondences play in our understanding of metaphoric expressions about love or, for that matter, our understanding of love as a concept?

According to the linguist George Lakoff, the correspondence between journeys and love is not simply a conventional linguistic strategy for talking about love but a mental structure that he refers to as a conceptual metaphor. The metaphor's existence is inferred from conventional love-journey expressions, but Lakoff asserts that the conceptual metaphor transcends its linguistic manifestations:

> What constitutes the LOVE IS A JOURNEY[1] metaphor is not any particular word or expression. It is the ontological mapping across conceptual domains, from the source domain of journeys to the target domain of love. The metaphor is not just a matter of language, but of thought and reason. The language is secondary. The mapping is primary, in that it sanctions the use of source domain language and inference patterns for target domain concepts. The mapping is conventional; that is, it is a fixed part of our conceptual system, one of our conventional ways of conceptualizing love relationships. (Lakoff, 1993, p. 208)

In this passage, Lakoff characterizes the conceptual metaphor that links love and journeys as playing two distinct but related roles: a representational role and a process role. It plays a representational role in that it structures our knowledge of love. The reasoning behind this claim is that the mind represents abstract concepts (such as love) in an economical fashion, borrowing the semantic structure of more concrete concepts (such as a journey) to organize aspects of the abstract concept. One reason for this is that it might be too computationally expensive to represent abstract concepts in a stand-alone fashion. Second, the love-journey metaphor plays a process role in that it mediates our use and understanding of journey-related metaphoric expressions pertaining to love. For example, upon encountering the statement *our relationship has hit a dead end*, we retrieve the fixed conceptual mappings between love and journeys (e.g., lovers-travelers, relationship-vehicle, problems—obstacles) to interpret the statement. Again, the metaphor's hypothesized process role appears to be economical from a computational standpoint, in that (a) metaphoric meanings may be retrieved rather than constructed de novo and (b) the meanings of any number of metaphoric expressions (e.g., dead end, spinning our wheels) may be generated from a single semantic structure (the love-journey conceptual mapping).

Lakoff and other cognitive linguists have used the theory of conceptual metaphors to describe the way that we think and talk about a variety of concepts, including anger (ANGER IS HEATED FLUID UNDER

PRESSURE, as in *Matt* **blew his stack**), crime (CRIME IS A DISEASE, as in *Midtown has been* **plagued** by a series of bank robberies), death (DEATH IS DEPARTURE, as in *The old man finally* **passed away**), mentality (THE MIND IS A CONTAINER, as in *What do you have in mind?*), and many others (Lakoff, 1987, 1993; Lakoff & Johnson, 1977, 1980; Lakoff & Turner, 1989; see also Kovecses, 1990). The theory has been extremely influential in linguistic scholarship and in other fields as well. Philosophers and linguists have used it to describe how our understanding of abstract concepts is embodied in our sensorial experience (Johnson, 1981, 1987; Talmy, 1996). Psychologists and artificial intelligence researchers have developed process models of figurative language comprehension in which cross-domain conceptual mappings figure prominently (Carbonell, 1982; Greiner, 1985, 1988; Way, 1991; Gibbs, 1992a, 1992b, 1994; Allbritton, McKoon, & Gerrig, 1995; Gentner & Markman in press). The theory has also had an impact on conceptions of the relationship between language and thought in such diverse fields as cultural anthropology (Holland, 1982; Quinn, 1991), literary studies (Turner, 1987, 1991; Steen, 1992, 1994), law (Winter, 1989), political science (Hallet, 1991), and religion (Soskice, 1990). Despite its widespread influence, however, the theory remains controversial within cognitive science. In the remainder of this chapter, I discuss the major issues that have been raised about conceptual metaphor theory. This discussion is presented in three sections. In the first section, I discuss how the theory's representational claim fares as an account of abstract conceptual structure. In the second section, I describe the empirical evidence pertinent to the theory's process claim. In discussing the evidence relevant to nominal metaphor processing, I contrast the conceptual metaphor theory with the property attribution model proposed by Glucksberg and his colleagues. Finally, in the third section I draw conclusions about the theory's promise as a comprehensive theory of figurative thought and language.

The Metaphoric Representation of Conceptual Structure

In his writings on the subject, Lakoff makes it very clear that he does not view metaphor as being solely (or even primarily) a linguistic phenomenon; rather, he considers it to be a mode of conceptual representation. Specifically, he argues that metaphor constitutes the primary method by which the mind represents concepts that are not sensorial or perceptual in nature:

> Many aspects of our experience cannot be clearly delineated in terms of the naturally emergent dimensions of our experience. This is typically the case for human emotions, abstract concepts, mental activity. . . . Though most of these can be experienced directly, none of them can be fully comprehended on their own terms. Instead, we must understand them in terms of other entities and

experiences, typically other kinds of entities and experiences. (Lakoff & Johnson, 1980, p. 177)

On this view, metaphor provides a way to representationally piggyback our understanding of abstract concepts on the structure of concrete concepts, which presumably are represented in their own terms, that is, in a stand-alone fashion.

While Lakoff stresses the role of metaphor in conceptual representation, neither he nor his colleagues have offered a detailed model of how meta-phoric representations are constructed or used. In the absence of an explicit model from proponents of the conceptual metaphor view, Murphy (1996, 1997) formulated two versions of what such a model might look like, a strong version and a weak version. In the strong version, all concepts other than those based directly on sensorial-perceptual experience have no in-trinsic structure of their own. Instead, they are represented entirely as a set of mappings from the representational structure of more concrete con-cepts. For example, consider the hypothesized conceptual metaphor THE-ORIES ARE BUILDINGS (Lakoff & Johnson, 1980). This metaphoric mental structure is inferred from idiomatic expressions such as *She con-structed a theory to explain the incident* and *That theory is on shaky ground.* According to the strong version, the structure of the theory concept is a set of argument-related entities that are organized by correspondences to entities in the concept of buildings:

Theory concept	Building concept
Theory	Building
Theorist	Builder
Formulation	Construction
Ideas	Materials
Assumptions	Foundation
Validity	Sturdiness
Revision	Renovation

The strong version assumes that we cannot reason about theories in and of themselves but must instead apply our knowledge of buildings to theory properties. Thus, this version suggests that we don't understand theories in any real sense; we can understand only buildings and must piggyback the theory concept on this understanding. Although Lakoff and his col-leagues do not explicitly endorse this version, they do make statements that are consistent with it. For example, Lakoff and Turner (1989) argue that conventional love-journey expressions demonstrate that the "structure of our understanding of life comes from the structure of our knowledge of journeys" (p. 62). Lakoff and Johnson's (1980, p. 5) claim that "the essence of metaphor is understanding and experiencing one kind of thing in terms of another" is also consistent with this view.

The strong version of the metaphoric representation claim is problem-atic for at least two reasons. First, it is not clear how the mind could construct such a representation without at least some semantic primitives in the abstract concept that exist independent of those in the concrete concept to which they metaphorically correspond. For example, we must have some direct representation of theory-related entities (e.g., theories themselves, theorists, ideas, assumptions) if they are to be distinguished from the building-related entities to which they conceptually correspond. Without at least a minimal independent representation of theories, we would assume that theory terms are synonymous with building terms and would be conceptually incapable of distinguishing between them. Second, the strong version requires that our knowledge of abstract concepts include incorrect information that is a by-product of their metaphoric structure (Murphy, 1996). Thus, if we understand theories entirely in terms of buildings, then we should occasionally make erroneous inferences about the applicability of building properties to the abstract concept—for example, that theories not only can have foundations (assumptions), architects (formulators), and blueprints (origins), but also have stairwells (?), hallways (?), sprinkler systems (?), and so on. People rarely, if ever, make inferences of this sort; however, someone whose concept of theories is entirely parasitic on her knowledge of buildings could learn to distinguish correct from incorrect inferences only through a lengthy (and unlikely) process of trial and error.

While the strong version of the metaphoric representation claim is theoretically untenable, Murphy's (1996) weak version might be more plausible. According to this version, abstract concepts are not exclusively piggybacked on concrete concepts but are nonetheless influenced by their conceptual structure. Metaphor still plays a role in organizing the abstract concept, but the representation of the abstract concept is not metaphorical per se. For example, our knowledge of theories may be represented independently, complete with semantic primitives that are intrinsic to theories and independent of our knowledge of buildings. However, the ubiquity of building-oriented idioms about theories in our culture may nonetheless have exerted an influence on our understanding of theories, resulting in a concept of theories that is similar in some relevant respects to our concept of buildings. The weak version thus assumes that metaphor plays a causal role in the structure of abstract concepts but is not the sine qua non of their conceptual representation.

In contrast to the strong version, the weak version of the metaphoric representation claim is open to empirical investigation. A reasonable test of the claim would, at a minimum, involve three steps. First, one would identify an abstract concept for which the set of idiomatic expressions in a particular culture suggests a conceptual metaphor, such as the THEORIES ARE BUILDINGS metaphor in our culture. Next, one would explore the idiomatic expressions used in another culture to describe the concept and determine whether this culture employs a different metaphor. Third, having established that members of the different cultures talk about theories in different ways, one would then seek to demonstrate that they think about theories in different ways, as evidenced by performance in nonlinguistic reasoning about theories. This third step is crucial, for without it there is no empirical basis for the claim that conceptual metaphors transcend their linguistic manifestations (Lakoff, 1993).

At present, however, conceptual metaphor research has not yet gone beyond the first step of the investigation. Lakoff and his colleagues base the metaphoric representation claim solely on intuitions about how certain idioms thematically cohere. As the sole evidence for the conceptual metaphor claim, the idiom corpus suffers from two serious problems. Consider, first, the early history of the Whorfian hypothesis, which clearly demonstrated the pitfall of using only linguistic evidence to argue for deep connections between thought and language (Glucksberg, 1988; Pullum, 1991). As is well known, Whorf (1956) argued that language influences thought by providing semantic distinctions and categories that people use to perceive and reason about objects and events in the world. However, the early evidence that was brought to bear on this hypothesis—differences in syntax and semantics among the world's languages—was exclusively linguistic. For example, Whorf's celebrated claim that Inuit speakers think of snow differently from English speakers rested entirely on the observation from which the claim was initially derived—that the Inuit language has more snow descriptors than English (as it turns out, even this claim is dubious; see Pullum, 1991). The linguistic evidence thus constituted both the motivation for the linguistic relativity hypothesis and its sole source of support (initially, at least[2])—a clear case of circular reasoning.

Analogously, Lakoff's claim that metaphors transcend their linguistic manifestations to influence conceptual structure rests solely on these manifestations. How do we know that people think of theories in terms of buildings? Because people often talk about theories using building-related expressions. Why do people often talk about theories using building-related expressions? Because people think about theories in terms of buildings. Clearly, the conceptual metaphor view must go beyond circular reasoning of this sort and seek evidence that is independent of the linguistic evidence.

A second problem with the linguistic evidence is that although it may be consistent with (if not force) the metaphoric representation claim, it may nonetheless be misleading. Our intuitions about how idioms metaphorically acquire their meanings are often quite compelling, even when they are dead wrong. The very act of generating an intuition about an idiom's meaning can make one resistant to alternatives accounts that may in fact be correct. Philological fixedness of this sort was demonstrated in a clever set of experiments by Keysar and Bly (1995). The people in their experiments studied a set of unfamiliar idioms, each of which was presented in one of two story contexts. For example, the archaic British idiom *the goose hangs high* was presented either in a story that biased people to interpret it as referring to success or in a different story that suggested that it refers to failure. After reading the idiom in one of these biasing contexts, people were asked to evaluate the likelihood that other people might interpret the idiom in the opposite manner if it were presented in isolation. Once people had learned one meaning for the idiom, they were less willing to accept the possibility that someone else might understand it in the opposite way. Keysar and Bly interpreted this finding as a form of hindsight bias (Fischoff, 1975) in which people developed a rationale for how each idiom metaphorically acquires its original meaning. Once this rationale was articulated, people were reluctant to consider a different metaphorical scheme that would just as easily justify the idiom's opposite meaning. For example, someone who was initially led to believe that *the goose hangs high* refers to success might assume that the metaphorical basis for its meaning is the conventional correspondence between "high" and positive feelings (e.g., HAPPY IS UP, SAD IS DOWN; Lakoff & Johnson, 1980). In contrast, someone who was initially led to believe that the idiom refers to failure might assume that the goose's death symbolizes failure (FAILURE IS DEATH; Johnson, 1987). Without knowledge of the idiom's actual etymology (the former account is in fact the correct one), both of these metaphoric schemes seem plausible but are incompatible with meanings of the idiom other than the ones they were designed to explain. Consequently, developing a theory about why an idiom metaphorically reflects its meaning can make people less receptive to alternative accounts of its meaning (Keysar & Bly, 1995).

This phenomenon—becoming convinced of an ambiguous expression's meaning once an interpretation has been made—is not limited to college students in laboratory settings. A case in point is provided by Steven Winter, a legal scholar who has written on the "correct" interpretation of a legal phrase, "under color of law" (Winter, 1992).[3] The phrase occurs in section 1983 of the federal act of April 20, 1987, that provides protection and redress for violations of the Constitution of the United States that are committed "under color of" state law. At issue is the interpretation of that phrase: does it mean under the legitimate authority of state law, or does it mean without authority or in violation of state law, merely having the *appearance* of legitimate authority? In a classic supreme court case, *Monroe v. Pape*, the court majority held to the latter meaning: under the *appearance* of law. In dissent, Justice Felix Frankfurter wrote that " '[u]nder color' of law meant by authority of law in the nineteenth century" (cited in Winter, 1992, p. 324). Winter argues in favor of the "appearance" interpretation, relying on two sources, legal precedent and cognitive linguistics. We are not competent to comment on Winter's legal arguments, but we can comment on his cognitive linguistic argument. Winter claims that the meaning of "under color of law" is motivated by two conventional conceptual metaphors. The first is HAVING CONTROL IS UP, with its corollary BEING SUBJECT TO CONTROL IS DOWN. The second is UNDERSTAND-

ING IS SEEING. The "under" rests on the first metaphor, the "color" on the second. Armed with this analysis, Winter concludes that "the phrase *under color of law* is an unlikely, even counterintuitive way in which to express the position advocated by Frankfurter. Rather a cognitive analysis of the metaphor demonstrates that it connotes something like 'under a deceptive appearance of authority' and that this meaning is *overdetermined*" (p. 385, emphasis in original).

We tested this hypothesis by asking twelve people to interpret the assertion "The property was foreclosed under color of law." If the "appearance of law" meaning is indeed overdetermined by the two conceptual metaphors cited by Winter, then at least a majority of our informants should have given that interpretation. We found just the opposite. Eleven people said that it meant under the authority of the law; one person also said that it meant under the authority of law but added that it involved taking advantage of a loophole in the law. And, of course, none of our respondents recalled having encountered the color-of-law phrase before. Clearly, the meaning of "under the color of law" is not overdetermined in the direction claimed and justified by Winter. The post hoc rationalization in terms of conceptual metaphors is just that: a rationalization and not a viable linguistic or cognitive analysis.

Proponents of the metaphoric representation claim interpret the idiomatic corpus in a manner similar to the post hoc rationalization process used by Winter and by the people in Keysar and Bly's experiment. The conceptual metaphor view assumes that our intuitions about idioms' meanings directly reflect the way these meanings are represented in semantic memory. However, introspections of this sort may be misleading. To illustrate, consider how our intuitions about the metaphorical structure of the idiom *the spitting image* might lead us to create an erroneous account of the phrase's origin. This idiom is used to refer to the striking physical resemblance of one person to another—for example, *Martha is the spitting image of her mother*. But how does the idiom metaphorically reflect this meaning? One might create an account in which the reference to a bodily fluid (*spitting*) is meant to symbolize the genuine, physical quality of the resemblance. Such an account is consistent with Johnson's (1987) arguments for the metaphoric grounding of psychological experience in bodily functions (e.g., *I couldn't swallow the idea* reflects a THINKING IS DIGESTION metaphor). Furthermore, the "bodily fluid" account is also compatible with the idiom's status as an impolite expression (Makkai, Boatner, & Gates, 1995). Nevertheless, this explanation of the idiom's origin is completely wrong. *The spitting image* actually originated as a contraction of the phrase *the spirit and the image* (Feldman, 1990). In this example, the availability of etymological information enables us to evaluate (and ultimately discredit) our intuitive theory about the expression's origin. Analogously, the claim that idioms reflect the metaphoric structure of abstract concepts cannot be objectively evaluated without evidence that is independent of our intuitions. At present, there is simply no evidence available for such an evaluation of the idiom corpus.

Conceptual Metaphors in Figurative
Language Comprehension

As Murphy (1996, 1997) argued, there is no evidence to support the strong or weak versions of the metaphoric representation claim. However, an even weaker version of this claim might merit consideration. On this version, metaphors such as THEORIES ARE BUILDINGS do not structure our understanding of theories in general (the strong version), nor do they exert an indirect influence on the structure of our theory knowledge (the weak version). Nevertheless, they are part of our knowledge of how people talk about such abstract concepts and can play an important role in our understanding of figurative expressions that refer to such concepts. In the field of psycholinguistics, Raymond Gibbs has been the major proponent of this version of the representation claim, which amounts to a *process* claim—that conceptual metaphors underlie the processes with which we interpret figurative language (Gibbs & O'Brien, 1990; Nayak & Gibbs, 1990; Gibbs 1992a, 1992b, 1994).

Gibbs has proposed that our comprehension of the vast majority of linguistic metaphors—both conventional and novel figurative expressions—is fundamentally a recognition process. Specifically, he argues that we understand figurative expressions by recognizing the conceptual metaphors that they instantiate. To illustrate, consider the statement *Our marriage is a roller coaster ride*. According to Gibbs, we comprehend this statement by first recognizing it as an instantiation of the conceptual metaphor LOVE IS A JOURNEY. We then use the conceptual mappings that this metaphor entails (e.g., lovers-travelers, relationship-vehicle, excitement-speed, positive affect-upward direction of travel, negative affect-downward direction of travel) to interpret the statement as an assertion that the marriage in question is emotionally unstable. These conceptual mappings are presumably retrieved to comprehend other love-journey expressions as well—for example, *Love is a two-way street; Our relationship is at a crossroads*.

This account of metaphor comprehension contrasts sharply with the property attribution model described by Glucksberg and his colleagues (Glucksberg, 1991; Glucksberg & Keysar, 1990; Glucksberg, McGlone, & Manfredi, 1997). According to this model, metaphors such as *Our marriage is a roller-coaster ride* are understood as what they appear to be: class-inclusion assertions of the form *X is a Y*. The vehicle term (*roller-coaster ride*) is understood as referring to a category that its literal referent exemplifies ("exciting and/or scary situations") and may plausibly include the topic concept (*our marriage*) as a member. When such a category is used to characterize a metaphor topic, it functions as an attributive category in that it provides properties that could be attributed to the topic.

The properties that could be provided by such a category can often be attributed to a wide range of topics. Thus, we can characterize things such as adolescence, careers, elections, or films as being metaphorical roller-coaster rides, just as certain marriages can be roller-coaster rides (recall the play *Who's Afraid of Virginia Woolf?*). With extensive use in metaphoric contexts, the vehicle's attributive category referent can become a conventional meaning of the term. For example, the secondary sense of the term *butcher* in the *Random House Dictionary of the English Language* is "to bungle or botch," which reflects the term's now-conventional use as a symbol of incompetence.

Gibbs and Glucksberg's models of metaphor comprehension differ in the degree to which they characterize metaphor comprehension as an active, constructive process. Gibbs argues that the meanings of the vast majority of linguistic metaphors are retrieved as prestored conceptual mappings. According to Glucksberg, the meanings of conventional metaphor vehicles (e.g., *butcher*) may be retrieved from semantic memory but nonetheless are actively instantiated in different and sometimes novel ways for different topics. Thus, understanding *my surgeon is a butcher* entails a different construal of the category of incompetent, bungling people than does understanding *my carpenter is a butcher*. For novel metaphors, Glucksberg assumes that we rely on our knowledge of the vehicle's stereotypical properties and the attributional dimensions of the topic to construct attributive categories de novo (Glucksberg, McGlone, & Manfredi, 1997).

McGlone (1994, 1996) used a variety of experimental paradigms to investigate whether people use conceptual metaphors or attributive category knowledge to interpret nominal metaphors. In general, the results of these experiments did not support the conceptual metaphor view. For example, consider the statement *Dr. Moreland's lecture was a three-course meal for the mind*, which could instantiate (hypothetically) the conceptual metaphor IDEAS ARE FOOD (Lakoff & Johnson, 1980). When people were asked to paraphrase this statement, they rarely made mention of the potential correspondences between ideas and food (e.g., thinking-cooking, understanding-digestion). Instead, they focused on the high-quantity and/or-quality aspects of three-course meals that can be attributed to lectures. When asked to generate other metaphors that were similar in meaning to this statement, people most often generated metaphor vehicles from the same attributive category as three-course meals (e.g., *Dr. Moreland's lecture was a goldmine of information*); only infrequently were these new vehicles from the food domain (e.g., *Dr. Moreland's lecture was a steak for the intellect*). Furthermore, people's perceptions of the similarities among metaphors did not reflect putative conceptual metaphoric groupings. For example, the *steak* expression was not seen as being more similar to the original *three-course meal* statement than the *goldmine* expression, even though the first two metaphors are both from the food domain. Similarly, people's comprehension of the *three-course meal* statement was not facilitated to a greater degree by prior exposure to metaphors from the food domain (e.g., *That book was a snack*) than to others from three-course meals' attributive category (e.g., *That book was a goldmine*). Finally, people's memory for the *three-course meal* statement was far better when a recall cue (a hint) referred to the vehicle's attributive category (*large quantity*) than when it referred to the conceptual metaphor's putative source domain (*food*). Taken as a whole, these findings, replicated with a wide range of metaphors, cast serious doubt on the claim that conceptual metaphors underlie people's comprehension of everyday, conversational metaphors. Instead, people appear to infer, articulate, and remember the attributive categories to which these metaphors refer.

As my analysis indicates, there are good reasons to doubt the role of conceptual metaphors in nominal metaphor comprehension. However, they may still play a role in idiom comprehension. While idioms cannot be taken as strong evidence that certain concepts are metaphorically structured (as I argued in the previous section), it is nonetheless possible that people can recognize the metaphoric coherence of idioms in certain linguistic domains and perhaps use this knowledge for understanding such idioms.

In this vein, Nayak and Gibbs (1990) found that people not only can recognize the metaphoric similarities among idioms but also can use this knowledge to make judgments about the relative appropriateness of idioms in discourse contexts. For example, consider the idioms that people use to discribe anger. Lakoff (1987) has described anger idioms as clustering around two distinct conceptual metaphors, ANGER IS HEATED FLUID UNDER PRESSURE and ANGER IS ANIMAL-LIKE BEHAVIOR. Idioms such as *flip your lid, blow your top*, and *get hot under the collar* are consistent with the former; others, such as *bite someone's head off, foam at the mouth*, and *jump down someone's throat*, are consistent with the latter. Using materials such as these, Nayak and Gibbs found that people base their judgments of the similarities among anger idioms in part on their metaphoric similarities. Thus, *flip your lid* was on average judged to be more similar in meaning to *blow your top* than to *jump down someone's throat*. In another study of such idioms, people judged the stylistic consistency of anger idioms in stories such as the following (emphases added):

> Mary was very *tense* about this evening's dinner party. The fact that Chuck had not come home to help was making her *fume*. She was *getting hotter* with every passing minute. Dinner would not be ready before the guests arrived. As it got closer to five o'clock *the pressure was really building up*. Mary's tolerance was reaching its limits. When Chuck strolled in at ten minutes to five whistling and smiling, Mary. . . .

After reading this vignette, people judged the relative appropriateness of *blew her top* and *bit his head off* as descriptions of Mary's angry behavior in the final sentence. *Blew her top* was overwhelmingly preferred as a completion for this vignette, while *bit his head off* was preferred for the following:

Mary was getting very *grouchy* about this evening's dinner party. She *prowled* around the house waiting for Chuck to come home to help. She was *growling under her breath* about Chuck's lateness. Her mood was becoming more *savage* with every passing minute. As it got closer to five o'clock, Mary was *ferociously* angry with Chuck. When Chuck strolled in at 4:30 whistling and smiling, Mary . . .

The appropriateness ratings that people gave for these and other idiom-vignette pairings clearly suggest that people can appreciate the metaphoric consistency of idioms in certain discourse contexts.

Nayak and Gibbs (1990) interpreted these data as reflecting the role that conceptual metaphors play in idiom comprehension. Specifically, they argued that the appropriateness ratings indicated the relative difficulty people had in comprehending the competing idiom completions. Idioms that metaphorically matched their story contexts—for example, *blew her top* in a story describing anger in heat and pressure terms—were easier to interpret than were idioms in nonmatching contexts. The appropriateness ratings, on this account, directly reflected the relative difficulty of idiom comprehension. There are, however, plausible alternative interpretations of these data. The pattern of idiom preferences that Nayak and Gibbs report is consistent with three different scenarios regarding the conceptual status of the ANGER IS HEATED FLUID UNDER PRESSURE metaphor. First, the metaphor might not be part of our prestored conceptual knowledge at all. It could be that we can simply appreciate how idioms imply a conceptual metaphor in interpretive contexts that motivate us to look for such metaphors, such as when we are specifically asked to rate the relative appropriateness of various idioms in select contexts. Second, the metaphor might be prestored in semantic memory and be available for use in processing idioms when appropriate occasions arise. In this scenario, the anger-heat equation is available in semantic memory and is accessed to understand *blew her top* in contexts that encourage consideration of the idiom's metaphoric underpinnings. Third, the metaphor might be available in semantic memory, ready to be accessed in any context in which anger-heat idioms are encountered, and thus might serve as the conceptual basis for idiom comprehension. Lakoff (1993) appears to endorse this third scenario when he suggests that the system of conceptual metaphors "is used constantly and automatically, with neither effort nor awareness" (pp. 227–228). However, people's ratings of idiom appropriateness is not sufficient to assess this strong processing claim.

To explore the hypothesized role of conceptual metaphors in idiom comprehension, Glucksberg, Brown, and McGlone (1993, Experiment 2) adapted the stories used by Nayak and Gibbs for use in a timed reading task. The vignettes were presented one line at a time on a computer screen, with either a metaphorically consistent idiom completion or an inconsistent completion. If conceptual metaphors are, as Lakoff (1993) argued, automatically accessed during reading, then subjects should have been able to read the metaphorically consistent idiom completions faster than the inconsistent completions. However, there were no differences whatsoever in reading times between the subjects' performance in the consistent and the inconsistent conditions. Gibbs (1992) reported a similar failure to find effects of metaphoric consistency on idiom comprehension performance as measured by reading times.

Other studies that have reported evidence to support Lakoff's (1993) strong processing claim are also open to alternative interpretations. For example, Allbritton, McKoon, and Gerrig (1995) explored the role of conceptual metaphors in people's memory for textual information. People read texts that contained metaphoric expressions that were potential instantiations of conceptual metaphors. For example, one text about urban crime read: *The city's crime epidemic was raging out of control.* It also stated: *Public officials desperately looked for a cure.* Both sentences presumably reflect the metaphor CRIME IS A DISEASE (Lakoff & Johnson, 1980). After reading such texts, people were given a recognition memory test. People were better at recognizing the first sentence when they were given the second, disease-related sentence as a cue than when they were given a comparable sentence that did not mention disease-related concepts. This result was taken to mean that during the original reading of the text, people established a link in memory between these two sentences because the sentences both instantiated the *CRIME AS DISEASE* metaphor. However, people might well have noticed such links even without recourse to such a conceptual metaphor. All that would be needed would be attention to thematic consistency and to the relation between such concepts as *epidemic* and *cure* (Kreuz & Graesser, 1991).

Despite the failure of these studies to demonstrate a functional role for conceptual metaphors in idiom comprehension, others have found convincing evidence of a relation between conceptual metaphors and comprehension. In one such study, McGlone and Harding (1998; see also McGlone, Harding, & Glucksberg, 1995, and Gentner, Imai, & Boroditsky, in press) investigated people's comprehension of temporal language. Linguists have long noted that two distinct movement perspectives are implicit in English expressions about temporal sequencing: one in which events are stationary relative to a moving observer (e.g., *We have passed the due date*) and a second in which events move relative to a stationary observer (e.g., *The due date has passed;* McTaggart, 1908; Anderson, 1971; Clark, 1973; Bennett, 1975). Lakoff (1993) has described these perspectives as special cases of the more general TIME PASSING IS MOTION metaphor that maps temporal relations to spatial relations. McGlone and Harding found that the entailments of these perspectives can play a role in language comprehension. First, people took less time to read and understand temporal sentences when they were presented in a perspectively consistent fashion (i.e., either all moving-observer or all moving-event sentences) than when the sentences were presented in a perspectively inconsistent fashion (i.e., moving-observer and moving-event sentences intermixed). Second, people used the perspectival information in unambiguous sentences to help them disambiguate ambiguous temporal sentences such as *The meeting originally scheduled for next Wednesday has been moved forward two days*. When people encountered this sentence following an unambiguous moving-observer sentence (e.g., *We passed the deadline two days ago*), they tended to interpret the term *forward* as indicating that the meeting had been postponed, consistent with a perspective in which the direction of temporal movement is toward the future. However, when the ambiguous sentence was encountered following an unambiguous moving-event sentence (e.g., *The deadline passed two days ago*), then they tended to interpret *forward* as indicating that the meeting had been moved earlier, consistent with a perspective in which events move from the future toward the past.

Do these data reflect use of different instantiations of the TIME PASSING IS MOTION metaphor? Perhaps, but this claim cannot be empirically distinguished from the more parsimonious claim that the moving-observer and the moving-event perspectives in temporal language are structurally similar to (but not metaphorically derived from) the moving-observer and the moving-object perspectives in spatial language. In a similar vein, Jackendoff (1983) argues that, although our conceptions of time and space may be thematically parallel (as illustrated by spatiotemporal expressions), the presumed primacy of spatial relations may be illusory. Spatial relations may *seem* primary because they involve concrete nonverbal cognitive operations such as those involved in seeing and moving about the world. Nevertheless, it is just as plausible to suppose that space, time, and other concepts are organized by a common set of abstract principles that are simply more transparent in spatial language than in other linguistic domains (Gruber, 1976; see also Talmy, 1996). Jackendoff's argument applies with equal force to the hypothesized role of conceptual metaphors in our understanding of conventional expressions in domains other than time and space. For example, the semantic and syntactic similarities among the conventional expressions that we use to describe anger (e.g., *John was fuming*) and heat (e.g., *The furnace is fuming*) might reflect the organizational influence of conceptual structures that are superordinate to both concepts. The semantic and syntactic similarities among these expressions may facilitate comprehension, consistent with the conceptual metaphor view. However, such facilitation effects might be attributable to such superordinate structures, rather than to the anger and/or heat concepts themselves.

While the evidence that conventional expressions are understood via conceptual metaphors is problematic, there is some evidence that people can spontaneously construct conceptual mappings to understand novel metaphoric expressions. Keysar, Shen, and Glucksberg (1998; see also Gentner & Boronat, 1992) reasoned that the novelty and explicitness of an expression might encourage readers to construct such mappings. For example, people probably don't need to use the mapping SAD IS DOWN to understand a conventional expression such as *I'm depressed*. However, the mapping might well be constructed for a novel utterance such *as I'm feeling lower than a piece of gum stuck on the bottom of your boots.* The novelty of the statement invites, perhaps requires, the reader to construct a metaphoric mapping between emotional state and elevation. To test this possibility, Keysar et al. presented vignettes to people that used either stock phrases or novel extensions of a conceptual mapping that was relevant to the meaning of a target metaphor. For example, the following vignette uses stock phrases that instantiate the mapping ARGUMENT IS WAR (emphases added):

> An argument follows the conduct of war. Stan and Jake argue whenever they get together. Stan always *strikes first, throwing his rival off balance.* But Jake keeps *his defenses up* and *shoots down* Stan's arguments. *Sirens wail every time they meet.*

In contrast, the version that follows employs novel ARGUMENT IS WAR expressions that might encourage people to construct a mapping:

> An argument follows the conduct of war. Stan and Jake argue whenever they get together. Stan always begins *the siege* by *launching his verbal grenades.* But Jake *keeps his barracks fortified* and *delivers a defensive strike. Sirens wail every time they meet.*

Keysar et al. found that people read the target sentence (*Sirens wail every time they meet*) faster when it followed the novel expression than when it followed the conventional vignette version. It is worth noting that both versions begin with a sentence that explicitly likens arguments to war, so the applicability of the conceptual metaphor to the target passage was transparent in both versions. Yet only the version with novel expressions appeared to facilitate interpretation of the target sentence.

Keysar et al.'s results support a straightforward claim regarding the role of conceptual metaphors in figurative language comprehension. People can understand stock expressions such as *the argument was shot down* without recourse to conceptual mappings such as ARGUMENT IS WAR. Stock expressions appear to be understood in the same way as are frozen metaphors such as *brake shoe*—directly and literally. In contrast, understanding novel expressions such as *Rush Limbaugh's bloated ego gobbled up his integrity and used the airwaves as a toilet* might very well involve inferring a conceptual mapping between arrogance and digestion. If you had previously encountered digestion as a metaphor for arrogance (which seems unlikely), then you could have retrieved this mapping, in theory, to understand the Limbaugh expression. If, on the other hand, you had never encountered this metaphor previously, then you would have had to create the mapping on the spot. As Bowdle and Gentner (1997) have suggested, the processes used to understand any particular metaphoric expression depend on its conventionality. When an expression is completely novel, it requires different kinds of inferential work than when it is familiar. Thus, the conceptual metaphor view is insufficient as a general account of figurative language comprehension, in part because it does not recognize important processing differences between conventional and novel expressions.

Conclusions

The conceptual metaphor view has been extremely influential in recent cognitive scientific research and theory. This influence has been valuable to the field in at least two respects. First, it has drawn much needed scholarly attention to the structure of abstract concepts (McGlone, 1996; Murphy, 1996). While cognitive researchers have traditionally focused on tidy natural-kind concepts such as *furniture, fruit,* and *vegetable,* cognitive linguists are among the few who have explored abstract concepts such as *anger, love, time, theories,* and *causality,* to name a few. Perhaps the debate over the representation and the process claims will lead to more research on these topics. Second, the conceptual metaphor view has generated renewed interest in how language structure might reflect conceptual structure (Gibbs, 1992). Although certain episodes (e.g., early explorations of the Whorfian hypothesis) in the history of this issue have been disappointing, the issue clearly warrants further attention (Lucy, 1992; Gumperz & Levinson, 1996).

Despite its valuable programmatic influence, the conceptual metaphor view has not fared well theoretically or empirically. There is an ironic quality to its shortcomings: while the view stresses the importance of metaphor in human cognition, one of its major shortcomings is its hyperliteral construal of the relationship between metaphoric language and thought. Consider Lakoff's metaphoric representation claim. Although the linguistic evidence can support only the limited claim that certain abstract and concrete concepts are thematically parallel (Jackendoff, 1983; Murphy, 1996; Ortony, 1988), Lakoff asserts that our knowledge of abstract concepts is quite literally subsumed by our knowledge of concrete concepts. A conceptual system designed this way, however, seems incapable of differentiating the literal from the metaphorical. For example, if one's knowledge of theories were entirely dependent on one's knowledge of buildings, then one should assume that theories are not merely metaphoric buildings but literal buildings! Lacking a concept of theories that is representationally independent from that for buildings, the system cannot think or talk about theories in and of themselves. Consequently, it would be incapable of appreciating the literal-metaphorical distinction. This scenario is clearly not a realistic portrayal of the human conceptual system, even though it follows directly from Lakoff and Johnson's (1980) assertion that abstract concepts are entirely parasitic on concrete concepts.

Literal-mindedness of this sort also underlies the hypothesized role of conceptual metaphors in figurative language comprehension. Consider the cues that a reader would have to use to recognize the conceptual metaphor relevant to understanding any particular linguistic metaphor. For example, to recognize that LOVE IS A JOURNEY is the relevant conceptual metaphor for *Our marriage was a roller-coaster ride*, the reader must construe *roller-coaster ride* as a reference to its literal superordinate category, "journey." However, the people in McGlone's (1996) paraphrase study did not interpret *roller-coaster ride* so literally; very few paraphrases referred to its journey-related properties. Roller-coaster rides as instances of journeys are quite irrelevant to the metaphor. Roller-coaster rides as instances of exciting, potentially scary events are relevant. Thus the properties of this category figured prominently in people's paraphrases of the metaphor. The generalization that follows from this example is that one cannot identify the ground of a metaphor from the literal, taxonomic category of the metaphor vehicle (Glucksberg & McGlone, 1999). In some cases, interpreting the vehicle in this way would be bizarre. For example, consider *My recent trip to L.A. was a roller-coaster ride*. If *roller-coaster ride* in this statement were to be interpreted as referring simply to a journey, then one would understand the statement as redundantly asserting that the trip in question was a journey! Clearly, no one would interpret this statement in such an inane manner. Our interpretation of this and other metaphor vehicles is not limited to their literal category memberships and more often than not transcends them.

Paradoxically, Lakoff couples this hyperliteral model of metaphor understanding to a hypermetaphoric construal of literal language. Many expressions that most people would consider literal are treated by Lakoff as metaphorical (Holland, 1982; Jackendoff & Aaron, 1991; Keysar, Shen, & Glucksberg, in press). For example, Lakoff (1993) argues that the statements *I have troubles* and *I'm in trouble* reflect the conceptual metaphors ATTRIBUTES ARE POSSESSIONS and STATES ARE LOCATIONS, respectively:

> In both cases, trouble is being attributed to me, and in both cases, trouble is metaphorically conceptualized as being in the same place as me (collocation)—in one case, because I possess the trouble-object and in the other case, because I am in the trouble-location. (p. 225)

An alternative to this metaphoric account of the statements' meanings is that words such as *have* and *in* are polysemous, capable of being used to refer to psychological states and attributes as well as to physical objects and locations. Jackendoff and Aaron (1991) note that such expressions lack the element of semantic incongruity that is typical of expressions that have been traditionally described as metaphors. For example, the concepts *love* and *journey* are semantically distinct, even though they share similarities that could conceivably motivate expressions such as *Our love has been an exciting journey*. In contrast, *states* and *locations* are not semantically distinct (i.e., being in a location is literally a type of "state"); consequently, characterizing *I'm in trouble* as metaphorical is distinctly odd.

This characterization is not only odd, but paradoxical. Metaphorical expressions are assumed to be understood in terms of their constituents' literal category memberships, yet our knowledge of these literal categories is assumed to be metaphorical at some deep level. By blurring the distinction between literal and metaphorical language, the theory becomes incoherent, both as a theory of language comprehension and as a theory of conceptual representation.[4]

Notes

Chapter 1

1. Author of *The Poetics of Mind* (1994), an excellent treatment of metaphor from a cognitive linguistics perspective.

2. The invisible ubiquity of metaphor might be illustrated by the two expressions in the immediately preceding text: *quickness* of tongue and metaphor *challenges*. Strictly (i.e., literally) speaking, tongues are not "quick," and abstract entities such as "metaphor" cannot "challenge" other abstract entities such as "definition."

3. Inherent in the notion of substitution is the assumption that metaphors are derivative of, and perhaps parasitic on, the literal language for which they substitute. See chapter 2 for a critical discussion of the primacy of the literal.

4. Richards (1936) introduced a useful set of terms for nominal metaphors. The metaphor "tenor" or "topic" refers to the subject noun and is considered to be the "given" information (Clark & Haviland, 1977). The metaphor "vehicle" is the predicate noun, and it provides the "ground" of the metaphor. The ground, in turn, is the new information provided by the vehicle, that is, the property or properties of the vehicle that are transferred to the metaphor topic. In the lawyer-shark example, "lawyer" is the metaphor topic, "shark" the metaphor vehicle, and properties such as predatory, aggressive, vicious, and tenacious constitute the ground of the metaphor. We will follow this convention here.

5. Dubois, Edelin, Klinkenberg, Minguet, Pire, and Trinon (1970), following traditional usage in rhetoric, refer to such tropes as *synecdoche*. I will follow contemporary usage introduced by Jakobson and Halle (1956) and refer to such tropes as instances of *metonymy*.

6. Jakobson and Halle (1956) drew a sharp distinction between paradigmatic substitution, as in genus for genus metaphors, and syntagmatic substitution, as in genus for species and species for genus ones. Whether there is a functional distinction between these two metaphor types remains to be seen.

7. This definition of meaning excludes entire classes of expressions, such as the performatives as discussed by Austin (1962). Performatives are expressions that accomplish something rather than assert something (e.g., a request such as "please close the door," a question such as "Is the door open?" or a social gesture, such as saying "thank

you"). These kinds of expressions have no meaning per se but instead are used to accomplish an end.

8. Not all philosophers of language share Davidson's view that semantics must be restricted to context-independent linguistic meanings. See, for example, Kittay (1987) and Stern (2000) for promising attempts to situate metaphorical meanings within semantic theory.

9. Actual instances of sentences, spoken or written, are referred to as "text" sentences. A "system" sentence is "an abstract, theoretical entity in the linguist's model of the language-system" (Lyons, 1977, p. 29).

10. If language users have no theory of language, then there should be no distinction between literal and nonliteral language use. Rumelhart (1993) observes that young children do not seem to distinguish between literal and metaphorical expressions, often coining their own metaphors (see Chukovsky, 1963, for wonderful examples of young children's spontaneous metaphor creations). In a similar vein, Rousseau observed that "figurative language was the first to be born. Proper [i.e., literal] meaning was discovered last" (cited in Stern, 2000).

Chapter 2

1. If literal meanings always require additional work to arrive at literal interpretations, then there is no reason to claim that literal meanings have priority. Instead, the claim would have to be about literal interpretations. If this is the case, then the priority of the literal would be not a natural consequence of how the language processor works but instead a consequence of a bias or preference for literal interpretations as a default strategy. We address this issue later in this chapter, where we consider the automaticity of metaphor processing.

2. Complete linguistic decoding may not be required in cases where an interpretation can be either generated or retrieved before the decoding is completed. For example, conventional idioms such as "spill the beans" might be understood before the phrase is fully parsed. In such cases, literal interpretations can take longer than figurative ones (Gibbs, 1983; McGlone, Glucksberg, & Cacciari, 1994).

3. Some writers (e.g., Bobrow & Bell, 1973) postulate a special "figurative processing mode, a predilection to interpret language figuratively rather than literally in certain contexts. Although this issue was not addressed directly in this study, the finding that literal contexts were as effective as figurative ones suggests that people do not need to be in any special "figurative processing mode" in order to understand metaphors quickly and automatically.

4. These conclusions do not apply to metonymic reference, which has been consistently found to take longer than literal reference (Gibbs, 1990). The reasons for this remain unclear.

Chapter 3

1. Feature salience depends on several factors. The most relevant in this context would be information value (i.e., how diagnostic it is of the concept). For example, the feature "crusty" would be diagnostic of French bread; the feature "sold in supermarkets" would not be particularly informative or diagnostic.

2. Similes that involve simple property attribution, such as *skyscrapers are like giraffes*, are reversible because the subject and predicate have the same salient feature, height relative to their surroundings. Therefore, we can say the reverse, *giraffes are*

like skyscrapers. There is still a subtle asymmetry. If we say that *skyscrapers are the giraffes of the city,* then the reversed statement must be changed to accommodate the difference between buildings and animals, yielding *giraffes are the skyscrapers of the African veldt.* Such similes may not even qualify as genus-for-genus metaphors. Unlike true metaphors, they do not seem as apt when paraphrased in metaphor form, as in *skyscrapers are giraffes* or *giraffes are skyscrapers.* They do, however, work well as analogies, as in *skyscrapers are to cities as giraffes are to jungles.*

3. In those few cases where metaphors seem reversible, they turn out to be, on closer analysis, implicitly reversed into their original order, as in *a mighty fortress is our God.* This is never taken to mean that a mighty fortress is an object of worship; rather, our god is (like) a mighty fortress.

4. Of course, one can almost always imagine a context in which any comparison could be informative. In the context of a conversation about mixed drinks, olives and cherries might be likened to each other because of their use in such drinks.

5. Interestingly, Ortony et al. (1985) did detect some salience imbalance in literal comparison statements as well (Study 3). It seems that people treat literal comparisons as informative statements in order to avoid trivial interpretations. If the properties that constitute the grounds for comparison are already high-salient in the *listener's* mental representation of both *a* and *b*, then that comparison statement simply repeats what the listener already knows. This repetition can be acceptable in one of two cases: the speaker may repeat something to remind the listener that a property is highly salient in the *a* term, as in "a cup is like a mug" when used as a reminder that cups and mugs can serve similar functions. Alternatively, the speaker can use a high-high match as an indirect speech act, to refer to something else. But *taken literally* as a high-high match, the comparison simply states the obvious and is therefore uninformative.

6. Bowdle and Gentner (1997) observe that "metaphoric comparisons . . . [have] greater levels of systematicity imbalance and directional informativity than are typically found in literal comparisons," but this can hardly serve as a reliable cue that a comparison is metaphorical rather than literal.

7. This is also the prescribed answer in the similarity subscale of a widely used IQ test, the Wechsler Adult Intelligence Scale (Wechsler, 1958). It is probably not coincidental that the most difficult items in the similarity subscale are those that belong to quite abstract and distant common categories (e.g., a fly and a tree, both living things).

8. When a less typical member of a category is used as the predicate in literal comparisons, then more specific properties may be inferred; for example, *ugli fruit is like a kiwi* would most likely be taken to mean that ugli fruit is small and green, tastes much like a kiwi, and probably grows in New Zealand.

9. In the spring of 1998, Yeltsin displayed erratic and potentially dangerous behaviors, including the summary discharge of his entire cabinet, followed by the reappointment of many members the following day. In this behavior he acted as a time bomb characteristically does: "exploding" at an unpredictable time and causing damage.

10. In classifier languages, nouns and verbs take forms that classify their referents in various ways. For example, ASL signers use two hands to trace the outline of symmetrical shapes but only one hand to describe an asymmetrical shape. The use of two hands or one "classifies" the shape as symmetric or asymmetric, respectively. Spoken classifier languages use prefixes, suffixes, or auxiliaries to classify referents according to properties such as shape, color, or size.

11. Generic use of brand names may be an efficient naming strategy for consumers, but it is the bane of their originators. If all copiers are called xerox machines, then the Xerox company loses a distinctive brand name. Small wonder that companies wage

extensive campaigns to educate consumers about the proper referential scope of a brand name. Consider, for example, Daimler-Chrysler Corporation's seemingly tautological admonition *Only a Jeep is a Jeep*. In recent years, the term *S.U.V.* (sports utility vehicle) has come into the popular lexicon to replace *Jeep*, a name that originated during World War II as slang for GP, a "general purpose" military vehicle. With the arrival of *S.U.V.*, the lexicon has come full circle.

12. Another common form of dual reference appears in colloquial tautologies such as "boys will be boys" (Gibbs & McCarrell, 1990). In this construction, the first use of "boys" refers to young human males, the second to the category of people who behave in stereotypical boy-like fashion (e.g., are rowdy, crude, insensitive, and immature). Viewed in this light, such constructions are not tautologies at all but informative attributive statements that use an ideal exemplar's name ("boys") to refer to the category that it exemplifies.

13. Identification of superordinate, basic, and subordinate levels is not fixed but can vary with level of expertise in a domain. For most people, *lettuce* is at the basic level. For an expert salad chef or for a gardener concerned with many different varieties of lettuce, *lettuce* is at the superordinate level, and *iceberg, romaine, Boston,* and *red-leaf* are at the level of usual utility as identified by Roger Brown in his classic paper "How Shall a Thing Be Called?" (Brown, 1958a).

14. A new superordinate category might even be given a name of its own, such as *rabbit food*, by people who need a convenient label to refer to the broader category of crunchy raw vegetables.

15. "Ideal" category members may be truly "ideal" in the sense that they literally do not have the characteristics of the metaphorical category that they represent. For example, gorillas are actually gentle and sweet creatures, and most people know this. Nevertheless, the metaphorical category *gorillas* is used to characterize people as aggressive, dangerous, and surly, as reflected in contemporary dictionary entries, where this meaning of "gorilla" is listed among its secondary senses.

16. Provided, of course, that the vehicle is relevant to, that is, informative about, the metaphor topic. For example, *lion* exemplifies nobility and courage in Western culture, and so *the soldiers defending their homeland were lions* would be apt, but *the apprentices working under the master painter were lions* would not be.

17. This example is analogous to John Demjanjuk's turning out not to be *A Demjanjuk*.

18. One reason that metaphors become conventional may be that they ideally represent their attributive categories. Perhaps the clearest examples of conventionalization are idioms such as *bury the hatchet* and *robbing Peter to pay Paul*. Burying a hatchet has become a prototypical symbolic action for ceasing hostilities and so can now be used to refer to any new member of that category, be it a domestic dispute or settling an old professional rivalry. *Robbing Peter to pay Paul* can similarly be used to refer to any form of temporary and ineffectual borrowing for the short term. These idioms act as do metaphors. They categorize their referents and by so doing characterize them in a nutshell, as it were.

19. These- *gates* refer, respectively, to the clandestine funding of CIA operations in Iran in 1985–1986; the disqualification of a nominee for a federal judgeship because she had employed a nanny for her children without withholding taxes or making the requisite social security payments; and President Clinton's alleged involvement in illegal real estate transactions when he was governor of Arkansas.

20. Both simple and systematic conventional metaphors are considered to be "metaphors we live by" (Lakoff & Johnson, 1980). These are conceptual metaphors that

underlie people's understanding of basic concepts such as love, time, communication and many—if not all—others. We consider conceptual metaphor theory in detail in chapter 6.

Chapter 4

1. Conventional metaphors are often listed in dictionaries as figurative senses. The *Oxford English Dictionary* lists "engage the full attention or interest of (a person); engross" as a secondary and figurative sense of *consume*, after its literal sense, "destroy by or like fire or (formerly) disease." In the example given here, both senses are commonly taken to be the intended meaning.

2. The interactive property attribution view we propose here is similar to that described by the philosopher Max Black (1962, 1979).

3. These predictions are at odds with Gentner's (1983) structural alignment model of metaphor comprehension. That model posits an initial stage of feature matching that should benefit from advance knowledge of either topic or vehicle, regardless of its characteristics. Feature matching cannot begin until features are first extracted from the topic and the vehicle. Advance presentation of any topic or vehicle should, therefore, be helpful because it permits a head start on feature extraction.

4. We included the vehicle terms in the topic-rating questionnaire and topic terms in the ambiguity assessment questionnaire to make sure that the dimensions of topic constraint and vehicle ambiguity were independent of each other. As we had expected, high- and low-ambiguous vehicles were equivalent in rated constraint level, 4.8 and 4.2 questions, respectively. High- and low-constraining topics were equivalent in rated ambiguity; both elicited a 28% agreement level.

5. The baseline mean response times for the four metaphor types were 2261 msec and 2321 msec for the high- and low-constraining topic metaphors, respectively, and 2284 and 2302 msec for the unambiguous and ambiguous vehicle metaphors, respectively.

6. Mean comprehension times for metaphors preceded by high- or low-constraint topics were 1445 and 2143 msec, respectively. Mean comprehension times for metaphors preceded by unambiguous or ambiguous vehicles were 1292 and 2330 msec, respectively.

7. Of course, all concepts can belong to some common category, such as "concepts." We have in mind here any natural kind category, such as birds, musical instruments, or fruits, of the sort used by Battig and Montague (1969).

8. Another sense in which property interpretation is interactive is that dimensions and features may become more or less relevant or salient, depending on the concept with which the property is combined. That is, a salient feature of a modifier may increase or even introduce the relevance of a dimension in the head concept, and vice versa. For instance, number of legs is not a particularly relevant dimension of *table*, since usually tables have four legs. However, that dimension becomes relevant in the combination *octopus table* when it is interpreted as a table with eight legs. This demonstrates that extremely high salience or relevance of one constituent may compensate for lower relevance or salience in the other constituent of a combination.

9. Gernsbacher et al. took this finding to suggest that metaphor-irrelevant properties are not merely not activated but may be actively suppressed during metaphor comprehension. This interpretation is consistent with Gernsbacher's (1990) structure-building model, as well as with the general class of models that posit inhibition as a mechanism for processing irrelevant information during discourse and text compre-

hension (cf. Hasher and Zacks, 1988; Gernsbacher and Faust, 1991; Kintsch, 1998; Simpson and Kang, 1994).

Chapter 5

1. At least in English, where the sound sequence TS in word-initial position is quite rare and is almost exculsively found in borrowed words such as zeitgeist and zigayne.

2. Because these quasi-metaphorical idioms have literal referents, they are often culture specific. If one did not know that Newcastle was a coal-mining city, then the idiom *carry coals to Newcastle* would make no sense. Then its meaning would have to be memorized. If the latter, then its meaning would be opaque.

3. I base this assumption on Miller and Johnson-Laird's observation that language understanding "occurs automatically without conscious control by the listener. [We] cannot refuse to understand . . ." (1976, p. 68), as well as on evidence of activation of literal meanings during idiom comprehension (Cacciari & Tabossi, 1988; Tabossi & Cacciari, 1988; Tabossi & Zardon, 1993, 1995).

4. The idiom *spill the beans* has become so conventional that the *American Heritage Dictionary of the English Language* lists, as one of the senses of the word *spill*, "To disclose (something previously unknown); divulge" (p. 1735).

5. Idioms may appear in variant form almost as often as in their original form, if examples from daily newspapers are any indication. On a page of the *New York Times* devoted to an economic and political crisis in Russia, the following two headlines appeared: "Can Old Russian Broom Sweep Economy Clean?" and "It's Hard to Even Find the Brass Ring on This Moscow Merry-Go-Round" (*New York Times*, August 24, 1998, p. A9). Nicolas (1995) examined a 50-million word corpus drawn from two daily newspapers and found that more than 85% of verb-noun phrase idioms allowed some form of internal modification.

6. Whenever there are exceptions to this rule (that one can always paraphrase an internal adjectival modifier adverbially), then the exception is relegated to the uninteresting wastebasket of word play and therefore is "external to the grammar of idioms" (p. 248). Examples of such word play are *Many people were eager to jump on the horse-drawn Reagan bandwagon* and *Bruce, a shark, found it* [a role in the film *Jaws*]) *a part he could really sink his three rows of teeth into* (Nicolas, p. 248, taken from Ernst, 1980, p. 52). From a psychological processing point of view, I find these examples no different in principle from Nicolas's so-called normal examples of internal modification. There seems to be nothing abnormal about the word play examples other than their not fitting into Nicolas's theoretical scheme. Apparently, when the shoe doesn't fit, throw out the foot! (But see Schenk, 1995, for a contrary view).

7. Most quasi-metaphoric idioms would be considered oligosemic by translation theorists because their meaning is embedded in the culture (Catford, 1965). Consider *go to bat for*. If one were not familiar with baseball and the role of pinch hitters, this idiom would be opaque. Similarly, *Catch-22* would be opaque to people unfamiliar with Heller's (1961) novel and his use of this phrase.

8. Mixed metaphors (and idioms) are often inadvertently produced because people take the literal meanings of the original expressions seriously, as in this prime example from a recent issue of the *Financial Times*: "Mr. Strauss-Kahn told the French National Assembly yesterday: 'Today everyone should know that Credit Lyonais is on its feet again; far from being garroted it is freed from the sword of Damocles that was weighing on its shoulders" (cited in the *New Yorker Magazine*, January 4, 1999).

9. The Dominican Republic is represented by players in the North American major leagues far out of proportion to its population. For example, more shortstops in the major leagues come from that country than from any other in the world.

Chapter 6

1. Lakoff (1993) uses uppercase titles to distinguish conceptual metaphors from their linguistic instantiations.

2. In recent years, some researchers have reported evidence suggesting that the structure of one's native language can influence performance in other cognitive, non-linguistic realms, such as perception or conceptual representation (see Gumperz & Levinson, 1996, for a review). However, the Whorfian hypothesis remains quite controversial.

3. We thank Lawrence Solan for calling our attention to this example.

4. By this judgment we do not intend to deny the role of metaphor in science and art or, more broadly, in society and culture. How we talk about the mind, art, people, or society both reflects and shapes how we think about these concepts. The argument developed in this chapter is explicitly narrow and is specifically focused on the conceptual metaphor theory in cognitive linguistics. Consideration of the complex relations between language and thought are beyond the scope of this book.

References

Agar, M. (1991). The biculture in bilingual. *Language-in-Society, 20*, 167–181.

Albritton, D. W., McKoon, G., & Gerrig, R. J. (1995). Metaphor-based schemas and text representations: Making connections through conceptual metaphors. *Journal of Experimental Psychology: Learning, Memory, and Cognition, 21*, 612–625.

American Heritage Dictionary of the English Language, 3d Ed. (1992). Boston: Houghton Mifflin.

Anderson, J. M. (1971). *The Grammar of Case: Towards a Localistic Theory*. Cambridge: Cambridge University Press.

Aristotle (1996). *Poetics*. Translated by Malcolm Heath. New York: Penguin Books.

Aristotle (1946). *Rhetoric*. Translated by R. Roberts. Oxford: Oxford University Press.

Austin, J. (1962). *How to Do Things with Words*. Cambridge, MA: Harvard University Press.

Barnes, K. (1998). *Brain dump on the blue badge: A guide to microspeak*. Cited in the *New York Times*, Aug. 13, p. G9.

Barsalou, L. (1983). Ad hoc categories. *Memory and Cognition, 11*, 211–227.

Barsalou, L. (1985). Ideas, central tendency, and frequency of instantiation as determinants of graded structure in categories. *Journal of Experimental Psychology: Learning, Memory, and Cognition, 11*, 629–654.

Barsalou, L. (1987). The instability of graded structure in concepts. In U. Neisser (Ed.), *Concepts and Conceptual Development: Ecological and Intellectual Factors in Categorization* (pp. 101–140). New York: Cambridge University Press.

Battig, W. F., & Montague, W. E. (1969). Category norms for verbal items in 56 categories: A replication and extensions of the Connecticut category norms. *Journal of Experimental Psychology Monograph, 80*, 1–46.

Bennett, D. C. (1975). *Spatial and Temporal Uses of English Prepositions: An Essay in Stratificational Semantics*. London: Longman Group.

Bierwisch, M. (1967). Some semantic universals of German adjectivals. *Foundations of Language, 3*, 1–36.

Black, M. (1962). *Models and Metaphors*. Ithaca, NY: Cornell University Press.

Black, M. (1979). More about metaphor. In A. Ortony (Ed.), *Metaphor and Thought* (pp. 19–43). Cambridge: Cambridge University Press.

Blasko, D. G., & Connine, C. M. (1993). Effects of familiarity and aptness on metaphor processing. *Journal of Experimental Psychology: Learning, Memory, and Cognition, 19*, 295–308.

Bobrow, S. A., & Bell, S. M. (1973). On catching on to idiomatic expressions. *Memory and Cognition, 1*, 343–346.

Bortfeld, H. (1997). A cross-linguistic comparison of idiom comprehension by native and non-native speakers. Unpublished doctoral dissertation, State University of New York at Stony Brook.

Bowdle, B. F., & Gentner, D. (1997). Informativity and asymmetry in comparisons. *Cognitive Science, 34*, 244–286.

Brown, R. (1958a). How shall a thing be called? *Psychological Review, 65*, 14–21.

Brown, R. (1958b). *Words and Things*. New York: Free Press.

Burke, K. (1945). *A Grammar of Motives*. New York: Prentice Hall.

Cacciari, C., & Glucksberg, S. (1991). Understanding idiomatic expressions: The contribution of word meanings. In G. B. Simpson (Ed.), *Understanding Word and Sentence* (pp. 217–240). Amsterdam, Netherlands: North-Holland.

Cacciari, C., & Tabossi, P. (1988). The comprehension of idioms. *Journal of Memory and Language, 27*, 668–683.

Camac, M., & Glucksberg, S. (1984). Metaphors do not use associations between concepts, they are used to create them. *Journal of Psycholinguistic Research, 13*, 443–455.

Caramazza, A., & Grober, E. (1976). Polysemy and the structure of the subjective lexicon. In C. Rameh (Ed.), *Georgetown University Round Table on Language and Linguistics* (pp. 181–206). Washington, DC: Georgetown University Press.

Carbonell, J. G. (1982). Metaphor: An inescapable phenomenon in natural language comprehension. In W. G. Lehnert & M. H. Ringle (Eds.), *Strategies for Natural Language Processing* (pp. 415–435). Hillsdale, NJ: Erlbaum.

Catford, J. C. (1965). *A Linguistic Theory of Translation*. London: Oxford University Press.

Chukovsky, K. (1963). *From Two to Five*, translated by M. Morton. Berkeley: University of California Press.

Clark, H. H. (1973). Space, time, semantics, and the child. In T. E. Moore (Ed.), *Cognitive Development and the Acquisition of Language* (pp. 27–63). New York: Academic Press.

Clark, H. H., (1996). *Using Language*. Cambridge: Cambridge University Press.

Clark, H. H., and Haviland, S. E. (1977). Comprehension and the given-new contract. In: R. O. Freedle (Ed.), *Discourse Production and Comprehension* (pp. 1–40). Norwood, NJ: Ablex.

Clark, H. H., & Lucy, P. (1975). Understanding what is meant from what is said: A study in conversationally conveyed requests. *Journal of Verbal Learning and Verbal Behavior, 14*, 56–72.

Cohen, B., & Murphy, G. L. (1984). Models of concepts. *Cognitive Science, 8*, 27–58.

Craig, C. (1986). Introduction. In C. Craig (Ed.), *Noun Classes and Categorization* (pp. 1–11). Amsterdam/Philadelphia: John Benjamins.

Cruse, D. A. (1986). *Lexical Semantics*. New York: Cambridge University Press.

Dascal, V. (1987). Defending literal meaning. *Cognitive Science, 11*, 259–281.

Davidson, D. (1977). What metaphors mean. In S. Sacks (Ed.), *On Metaphor* (pp. 29–45). Chicago: University of Chicago Press.

Denny, J. P. (1986). The semantic role of noun classifiers. In C. Craig (Ed.), *Noun*

Classes and Categorization (pp. 297–398). Amsterdam/Philadelphia: John Benjamins.

Donne, J. (c. 1635). "Hymn to God My God, in My Sickness." *Poems*. London.

Dubois, J., Edelin, F., Klinkenberg, J. M., Minguet, P., Pire, F., & Trinon, H. (1970). *Rhetorique generale*. Paris: Larousse.

Engel, M. (1996). Loose cannons, the horses's mouth and the bottom line: idioms and culture change. Paper presented at the XXVI International Congress of Psychology, Montreal, Canada.

Ernst, T. (1980). Grist for the linguistic mill: Idioms and "extra" adjectives. Paper presented at the Linguistic Society of America Annual Meeting, San Antonio, TX.

Estes, Z., & Glucksberg, S. (2000 a). Interactive property attribution in concept combination. *Memory and Cognition, 28*, 28–34.

Estes, Z., & Glucksberg, S. (2000 b). Similarity and attribution in concept combination: Reply to Wisniewski. *Memory and Cognition, 28*, 39–40.

Feldman, D. (1990). *Who Put the Butter in Butterfly? . . . and Other Fearless Investigations into Our Illogical Language*. New York: Harper Collins.

Fischoff, B. (1975). Hindsight does not equal foresight: The effect of outcome knowledge on judgment under uncertainty. *Journal of Experimental Psychology: Human Perception and Performance, 1*, 288–299.

Fodor, J. A. (1983). *The Modularity of Mind*. Cambridge, MA: Bradford Books.

Frazier, L. (1987). Theories of sentence processing. In J. L. Garfield (Ed.), *Modularity in Knowledge Representation and Natural Language Understanding* (pp. 291–307). Cambridge, MA: MIT Press.

Gagne, C. L., & Shoben, E. J. (1997). Influence of thematic relations on the comprehension of modifier-noun combinations. *Journal of Experimental Psychology: Learning, Memory, and Cognition, 23*, 71–87.

Galinsky, A. D., & Glucksberg, S. (2000). Inhibition of the literal: Metaphors and idioms as judgmental primes. *Social Cognition, 18*, 35–54.

Gentner, D. (1983). Structure-mapping: A theoretical framework for analogy. *Cognitive Science, 7*, 155–170.

Gentner, D., and Boronat, C. B. (1992). Metaphor as mapping. Paper presented at the Workshop on Metaphor, Department of Comparative Literature, Tel Aviv University.

Gentner, D., Imai, M., & Boroditsky, L. (in press). As time goes by: Evidence for two systems in processing space-time metaphors. *Language and Cognitive Processes*.

Gentner, D., & Markman, A. (1994). Structural alignment in comparison—No difference without similarity. *Psychological Science, 5*, 152–158.

Gentner, D., & Markman, A. B. (in press). Structure-mapping in analogy and similarity [Special issue]. *American Psychologist*.

Gentner, D., & Wolff, P. (1997). Alignment in the processing of metaphor. *Journal of Memory and Language, 37*, 331–355.

Gernsbacher, M. A. (1990). *Language Comprehension as Structure Building*. Hillsdale, NJ: Erlbaum.

Gernsbacher, M. A., & Faust, M. E. (1991). The mechanism of suppression: A component of general comprehension skill. *Journal of Experimental Psychology: Learning, Memory, and Cognition, 17*, 245–262.

Gernsbacher, M. A., Keysar, B., & Robertson, R. R. (1995). The role of suppression in metaphor interpretation. Paper presented at meetings of the Psychonomic Society, Los Angeles, CA.

Gerrig, R. J., & Healy, A. F. (1983). Dual processes in metaphor understanding: Comprehension and appreciation. *Journal of Experimental Psychology: Learning, Memory and Cognition, 9,* 667–675.

Gibbs, R. W. (1980). Spilling the beans on understanding and memory for idioms in conversation. *Memory and Cognition, 8,* 149–156.

Gibbs, R. W. (1983). Do people always process the literal meanings of indirect requests? *Journal of Experimental Psychology: Learning, Memory, and Cognition, 9,* 524–533.

Gibbs, R. W. (1984). Literal meaning and psychological theory. *Cognitive Science, 8,* 275–304.

Gibbs, R. W. (1990). Comprehending figurative referential descriptions. *Journal of Experimental Psychology: Learning, Memory, and Cognition, 16,* 56–66.

Gibbs, R. W. (1992a). Categorization and metaphor understanding. *Psychological Review, 99,* 572–577.

Gibbs, R. W. (1992b). What do idioms really mean? *Journal of Memory and Language, 31,* 485–506.

Gibbs, R. W (1993). Process and products in making sense of tropes. In A. Ortony (Ed.), *Metaphor and Thought* (2d Ed.) pp. 252–276). New York: Cambridge University Press.

Gibbs, R. W. (1994). *The Poetics of Mind: Figurative Thought, Language and Understanding.* New York: Cambridge University Press.

Gibbs, R. W., & McCarrell, N. (1990). Why boys will be boys and girls will be girls: Understanding colloquial tautologies. *Journal of Psycholinguistic Research, 19,* 125–145.

Gibbs, R. W., & Nayak, N. P. (1989). Psycholinguistic studies on the syntactic behavior of idioms. *Cognitive Psychology, 21,* 100–138.

Gibbs, R. W., & O'Brien, J. (1990). Idioms and mental imagery: The metaphorical motivation of idiomatic meaning. *Cognition, 36,* 35–68.

Gibbs, R. W., Nayak, N. P., & Cutting, C. (1989). How to kick the bucket and not decompose: Analyzability and idiom processing. *Journal of Memory and Language, 28,* 576–593.

Gibbs, R. W., Nayak, N. P., Bolton, J. L, & Keppel, M. E. (1989). Speakers' assumptions about the lexical flexibility of idioms. *Memory and Cognition, 17,* 58–68.

Gildea, P., and Glucksberg, S. (1983). On understanding metaphor: The role of context. *Journal of Verbal Learning and Verbal Behavior, 22,* 577—590.

Giora, R. (1997). Understanding figurative and literal language: The graded salience hypothesis. *Cognitive Linguistics, 7,* 183–206.

Giora, R. (in press). *On Our mind: Salience, Context, and Figurative Language.* New York: Oxford University Press.

Glucksberg, S. (1988). Language and thought. In R. Sternberg & E. E. Smith (Eds.), *The Psychology of Human Thought.* Cambridge: Cambridge University Press, pp. 214–241.

Glucksberg, S. (1991). Beyond literal meanings: The psychology of allusion. *Psychological Science, 2,* 146–152.

Glucksberg, S. (1993). Idiom meanings and allusional content. In C. Cacciari and P. Tabossi (Eds.), *Idioms: Processing, Structure, and Interpretation* (pp. 3–26). Hillsdale, NJ: Erlbaum.

Glucksberg, S., & Keysar, B. (1990). Understanding metaphorical comparisons: Beyond similarity. *Psychological Review, 97,* 3–18.

Glucksberg, S., & Keysar, B. (1993). How metaphors work. In A. Ortony (Ed.), Metaphor and Thought (2d Ed.) (pp. 401–424). New York, Cambridge University Press.

Glucksberg, S., & McGlone, M. S. (1999). When love is not a journey: What metaphors mean. *Journal of Pragmatics, 31,* 1541–1558.

Glucksberg, S., Brown, M. E., & McGlone, M. S. (1993). Conceptual analogies are not automatically accessed during idiom comprehension. *Memory and Cognition, 21,* 711–719.

Glucksberg, S., Gildea, P., and Bookin, H. A. (1982). On understanding nonliteral speech: Can people ignore metaphors? *Journal of Verbal Learning and Verbal Behavior, 21,* 85–98.

Glucksberg, S., Keysar, B., & McGlone, M. S. (1992). Metaphor understanding and accessing conceptual schemas: Reply to Gibbs (1992). *Psychological Review, 99,* 578–581.

Glucksberg, S., McGlone, M. S., & Manfredi, D. (1997). Property attribution in metaphor comprehension. *Journal of Memory and Language, 36,* 50–67.

Glucksberg, S., & Newsome, M. R., & Goldvarg, Y. (1997). Filtering out irrelevant material during metaphor comprehension. In M. G. Shafto & P. Langley (Eds.), *Proceedings of the 19th Annual Conference of the Cognitive Science Society,* Mahwah, NJ: Erlbaum, p. 932.

Goldvarg, Y., & Glucksberg, S. (1998). Conceptual combinations: The role of similarity. *Metaphor and Symbol, 13,* 243–255.

Goodman, N. (1972). *Problems and Projects.* New York: Bobbs-Merrill.

Greenberg-Concool, N. (1990). Idiom learning in young children. Unpublished manuscript, Princeton University.

Greiner, B. (1985). Dramatik der Zeichen: Botho Strauss-Trilogie des Weidersehens. *Text/Kontext, 13,* 158–176.

Greiner, R. (1988). Abstraction-based analogical inference. In D. H. Herman (Ed.), *Analogical Reasoning* (pp. 147–170). New York: Kluwer Academic.

Grice, H. P. (1975). Logic and conversation. In P. Cole & J. Morgan (Eds.), *Syntax and Semantics.* Vol. 3. *Speech Acts* (pp. 41–58). New York: Academic Press.

Gruber, J. S. (1976). *Lexical Structures in Syntax and Semantics.* Amsterdam: North Holland Press.

Gumperz, J. J., & Levinson, S. (1996). *Rethinking Linguistic Relativity.* Cambridge: Cambridge University Press.

Hage, P., and Miller, W. R. (1976). "Eagle" = "bird": A note on the structure and evolution of shoshoni ethnoornithological nomenclature. *American Ethnologist, 3,* 481–488.

Hallet, B. (1991). *Engulfed in War: Just War and the Persian Gulf.* Honolulu: Matsunaga Institute for Peace.

Hamblin J. L. & Gibbs, R. W. (1999). Why you can't kick the bucket as you slowly die: Verbs in idiom comprehension. *Journal of Psycholinguistic Research, 28,* 25–39.

Harris, R. (1976). Comprehension of metaphors: A test of the two-stage processing model. *Bulletin of the Psychonomic Society, 8,* 312–314.

Hasher, L., & Zacks, R. T. (1988). Working memory, comprehension, and aging: A review and a new view. In G. G. Bower (Ed.), *The Psychology of Learning and Motivation,* Vol. 22. (pp. 193–225). San Diego, CA: Academic Press.

Heller, J. (1961). *Catch-22.* New York: Modern Library.

Hendrickson, R. (1997). *Word and Phrase Origins* (Revised and expanded edition). New York: Facts on File.

Hirsch, E. D. (1988). *Cultural Literacy: What Every American Needs to Know.* New York: Vintage Books.

Holland, D. (1982). All Is Metaphor: Conventional Metaphors in Thought and Language. *Reviews in Anthropology, 9,* 287–297.

Horman, H. (1983). The calculating listener or how many are *einige, mehrere,* and *ein paar* (some, several, and a few). In R. Bauerke, C. Schwarze, & A. van Strechan (Eds.), *Meaning, Use, and Interpretation of Language* (pp. 221–234). Berlin: De Guyter.

Inhoff, A., Lima, S., & Carroll, P. (1984). Contextual effects on metaphor comprehension in reading. *Memory and Cognition, 12,* 558–567.

Jackendoff, R. (1983). *Semantics and Cognition.* Cambridge, MA: MIT Press.

Jackendoff, R. (1995). The boundaries of the lexicon. In M. Everaert, E. van den Linden, A. Schenk & R. Schreuder (Eds.), *Idioms: Structural and Psychological Perspectives* (pp. 133–166). Hillsdale, NJ: LEA.

Jackendoff, R., & Aaron, D. (1991). Review of *More than cool reason: A field guide to poetic metaphor. Language, 67,* 320–338.

Jakobson, R., & Halle, M. (1956). *Fundamentals of Language.* The Hague: Mouton.

Janus, R. A., & Bever, T. G. (1985). Processing of metaphoric language: An investigation of the three-stage model of metaphor comprehension. *Journal of Psycholinguistic Research, 14,* 473–487.

Johnson, M. (1981). *Philosophical Perspectives on Metaphor.* Minneapolis: University of Minnesota Press.

Johnson, M. (1987). *The Body in the Mind: The Bodily Basis of Meaning.* Chicago: University of Chicago Press.

Johnson, M. G., & Malgady, R. G. (1979). Some cognitive aspects of figurative language: Association and metaphor. *Journal of Psycholinguistic Research, 8,* 249–265.

Johnson-Laird, P. N. (1993). Foreword to C. Cacciari & P. Tabossi (Eds.), *Idioms: Processing, Structure, and Interpretation* (pp. vii–x). Hillsdale, NJ: LEA.

Keysar, B. (1989). On the functional equivalence of literal and metaphorical interpretations in discourse. *Journal of Memory and Language, 28,* 375–385.

Keysar, B., & Bly, B. (1995). Intuitions about the transparency of idioms: Can one keep a secret by spilling the beans? *Journal of Memory and Language, 34,* 89–109.

Keysar, B., & Bly, B. (1999). Swimming against the current: Do idioms reflect conceptual structure? *Journal of Pragmatics, 31,* 1559–1578.

Keysar, B., Shen, Y., Glucksberg, S., & Horton, W. S. (in press). Conventional language: How metaphorical is it? *Journal of Memory and Language.*

Kintsch, W. (1998). *Comprehension: A Paradigm for Cognition.* New York: Cambridge University Press.

Kittay, E. V. (1987). *Metaphor: Its Cognitive Force and Linguistic Structure.* Oxford: Clarendon Press.

Kovecses, Z. (1990). *Emotion Concepts.* New York: Springer-Verlag.

Kreuz, R. J., & Graesser, A. C. (1991). Aspects of idiom comprehension: Comment on Nayak and Gibbs. *Journal of Experimental Psychology: General, 120,* 90–92.

Lakoff, G. (1980). The metaphorical structure of the human conceptual system. *Cognitive Science, 4,* 195–208.

Lakoff, G. (1987). *Women, Fire, and Dangerous Things.* Chicago: University of Chicago Press.

Lakoff, G. (1990). The invariance hypothesis: Is abstract reasoning based on image-schemas? *Cognitive Linguistics, 1,* 39–74.

Lakoff, G. (1993). The contemporary theory of metaphor. In A. Ortony (Ed.), *Metaphor and Thought* (2d Ed.). Cambridge: Cambridge University Press, pp. 202–251.

Lakoff, G., & Johnson, M. (1977). Conceptual metaphor in everyday language. *Journal of Philosophy*, 77, 453–486.

Lakoff, G., & Johnson, M. (1980). *Metaphors We Live By*. Chicago: University of Chicago Press.

Lakoff, G., & Turner, M. (1989). *More than Cool Reason: A Field Guide to Poetic Metaphor*. Chicago: University of Chicago Press.

Lehrer, A. (1978). Structures of the lexicon and transfer of meaning. *Lingua*, 45, 95–123.

Levi, J. N. (1978). *The Syntax and Semantics of Complex Nominals*. New York: Academic Press.

Lucy, J. (1992). *Grammatical categories and cognition*. Cambridge: Cambridge University Press.

Lyons, J. (1977). *Semantics*. Cambridge: Cambridge University Press.

Makkai, A., Boatner, M. T., & Gates, J. E. (1995). *Dictionary of American Idioms*. Los Angeles: Barrons Educational.

Marschark, M., Katz, A., and Paivio, A. (1983). Dimensions of metaphor. *Journal of Psycholinguistic Research*, 12, 17–40.

Marslen-Wilson, W. D. (1987). Functional parallelism in spoken word recognition. *Cognitive Psychology*, 25, 71–102.

Marslen-Wilson, W., & Welsh, A. (1978). Processing interactions during word-recognition in continuous speech. *Cognitive Psychology*, 10, 29–63.

McClelland, J. L., & Elman, J. L. (1986). The TRACE model of speech perception. *Cognitive Psychology*, 18, 1–86.

McCloskey, M., & Glucksberg, S. (1978). Natural categories: Well-defined or fuzzy sets? *Memory and Cognition*, 6, 462–472.

McElree, B., & Griffith, T. (1995). Syntactic and thematic processing in sentence comprehension: Evidence for a temporal dissociation. *Journal of Experimental Psychology: Learning, Memory, and Cognition*, 21, 134–157.

McElree, B., & Griffith, T. (1998). Structural and lexical constraints on filling gaps during sentence comprehension: A time-course analysis. *Journal of Experimental Psychology: Learning, Memory, and Cognition*, 24, 432–460.

McElree, B., & Nordlie, J. (1999). Literal and figurative interpretations are computed in parallel. *Psychonomic Bulletin and Review*, 6, 486–494.

McGlone, M. S. (1994). Love, journeys, and traveling things: Analogies, metaphors, and categories. Unpublished doctoral dissertation, Princeton University.

McGlone, M. S. (1996). Conceptual metaphors and figurative language interpretation: Food for thought? *Journal of Memory and Language*, 35, 544–565.

McGlone, M. S., & Harding, J. L. (1998). Back (or forward?) to the future: The role of perspective in temporal language comprehension. *Journal of Experimental Psychology: Learning, Memory, and Cognition*, 24, 1–13.

McGlone, M. S., & Manfredi, D. (in press). Topic-vehicle interaction in metaphor comprehension. *Journal of Memory and Language*.

McGlone, M. S., Glucksberg, S., & Cacciari, C. (1994). Semantic productivity and idiom comprehension. *Discourse Processes*, 17, 167–190.

McGlone, M. S., Harding, J. L., & Glucksberg, S. (1995). Time marches on: Understanding time-as-movement expressions. In L. Vieu & P. Amsili (Eds.), *Time, Space, and Movement: Meaning and Knowledge in the Sensible World* (pp. 71–74). Toulouse, France: Groupe LRC.

McTaggart, J. M. E. (1908). The unreality of time. *Mind, 17,* 457–474.

Meyer, D. E., Schvaneveldt, R. W., & Ruddy, M. G. (1975). Loci of contextual effects on visual word recognition. In P. M. A. Rabbitt & S. Dornic (Eds.), *Attention and Performance,* Vol. 5. London: Academic Press.

Miller, G. A., & Glucksberg, S. (1988). Psycholinguistic aspects of semantics and pragmatics. In D. Luce, R. A. Atkinson, and R. Herrnstein (Eds.), *Steven's Handbook of Experimental Psychology* (2nd Ed.) (pp. 417–472). New York: Wiley.

Miller, G. A., & Johnson-Laird, P. (1976). *Language and Perception.* Cambridge, MA: Harvard University Press.

Minsky, M. (1975). A framework for representing knowledge. In P. H. Winston (Ed.), *The Psychology of Computer Vision,* (pp. 211–277). New York: McGraw-Hill.

Moliere, F. (1675). *Les Oeuvres de Monsieur Moliere.* Amsterdam: Elsevier.

Murphy, G. L. (1988). Comprehending complex concepts. *Cognitive Science, 12,* 529–562.

Murphy, G. L. (1990). Noun phrase interpretation and conceptual combination. *Journal of Memory and Language, 29,* 259–288.

Murphy, G. L. (1996). On metaphoric representation. *Cognition, 60,* 173–186.

Murphy, G. L. (1997). Reasons to doubt the present evidence for metaphoric representation. *Cognition, 62,* 99–108.

Nayak, N. P., & Gibbs, R. W. (1990). Conceptual knowledge in the interpretation of idioms. *Journal of Experimental Psychology: General, 119,* 315–330.

Newport, E. L., & Bellugi, U. (1978). Linguistic expressions of category levels in a visual-gesture language: A flower is a flower is a flower. In E. Rosch & B. B. Lloyd (Eds.), *Cognition and Categorization* (pp. 49–71). Hillsdale, NJ: Erlbaum,

Newsome, M. R. (1999). Property activation and inhibition during metaphor comprehension. Unpublished doctoral dissertation, Princeton University.

Nicolas, T. (1995). Semantics of idiom modification. In M. Everaert, E. van der Linden, A. Schenk, & R. Schreuder (Eds.), *Idioms: Structural and Psychological Perspectives* (pp. 233–252). Hillsdale, NJ: LEA.

Nunberg, G. (1978). *The Pragmatics of Reference.* Bloomington: Indiana University Linguistics Club.

Nunberg, G. (1979). The non-uniqueness of semantic solutions: Polysemy. *Linguistics and Philosophy, 3,* 143–184.

Onifer, W., & Swinney, D. A. (1981). Accessing lexical ambiguity during sentence comprehension: Effects of frequency of meaning and contextual bias. *Memory and Cogntion, 9,* 225–236.

Onishi, K. H., & Murphy, G. L. (1993). Metaphoric reference: When metaphors are not understood as easily as literal expressions. *Memory and Cognition, 21,* 763–772.

Ortega y Gasset, J. (1948). *The Dehumanization of Art.* New York: P. Smith.

Ortony, A. (1979). Beyond Literal Similarity. *Psychological Review, 86,* 161–180.

Ortony, A. (1988). Are emotion metaphors conceptual or lexical? *Cognition and Emotion, 2,* 95–103.

Ortony, A. (1993). Metaphor: A multidimensional problem. In A. Ortony (Ed.), *Metaphor and Thought* (2d Ed.) (pp. 1–16). Cambridge: Cambridge University Press.

Ortony, A., Schallert, D., Reynolds, R., & Antos, S. (1978). Interpreting metaphors and idioms: Some effects of context on comprehension. *Journal of Verbal Learning and Verbal Behavior, 17,* 465–477.

Ortony, A., Vondruska, R. J., Foss, M. A., & Jones, L. E. (1985). Salience, similes, and the asymmetry of similarity. *Journal of Memory and Language, 24,* 569–594.

Oxford American Dictionary (1980). New York: Oxford University Press (CD-ROM).

Oxford English Dictionary (1996). Oxford: Oxford University Press.

Potts, G. R., Keenan, J. M., & Golding, J. M. (1988). Assessing the occurrence of elaborative inferences: Lexical decision versus naming. *Journal of Memory and Language, 27*, 399–415.

Pullum, G. (1991). *The Great Eskimo Vocabulary Hoax and Other Irreverent Essays on the Study of Language*. Chicago: University of Chicago Press.

Pynte, J., Besson, M., Robichon, F. H., & Poli, J. (1996). The time-course of metaphor comprehension: An event-related potential study. *Brain and Language, 55*, 293–316.

Quinn, N. (1991). The cultural basis of metaphor. In J. W. Fernandez (Ed.), *Beyond Metaphor: The Theory of Tropes in Cultural Anthropology*. Stanford: Stanford University Press, pp. 56–93.

Random House Dictionary of the English Language. New York: Random House.

Ratcliff, R., & McKoon, G. (1986). Automatic activation of episodic information in a semantic memory task. *Journal of Experimental Psychology: Learning, Memory, and Cognition, 12*, 108–115.

Richards, I. A., (1936). *The Philosophy of Rhetoric*. New York: Oxford University Press.

Rosch, E. (1973). On the internal structure of perceptual and semantic categories. In T. E. Moore (Ed.), *Cognitive Development and the Acquisition of Language* (pp. 111–144). New York: Academic Press.

Rosch, E. (1978). Principles of Categorization. In E. Rosch & B. B. Lloyd (Eds.), *Cognition and Categorization* (pp. 27–48). Hillsdale, NJ: Erlbaum.

Roth, P. (1994). *Sabbath's Theater*. Boston: Houghton Mifflin.

Rumelhart, D. E. (1980). Schemata: The building blocks of cognition. In R. J. Spiro, B. C. Bruce, & W. F. Brewer (Eds.), *Theoretical Issues in Reading Comprehension* (pp. 33–58). Hillsdale, NJ: Erlbaum.

Rumelhart, D. (1993). Some problems with the notion of literal meanings. In A. Ortony (Ed.), *Metaphor and Thought* (2d Ed.) (pp. 78–90). New York: Cambridge University Press.

Sadock, J. M. (1993). Figurative speech and linguistics. In A. Ortony (Ed.), *Metaphor and Thought* (2d. Ed.) (pp. 42–57). New York: Cambridge University Press.

Schenk, A. (1995). The syntactic behavior of idioms. In M. Everaert, E. van den Linden, A. Schenk & R. Schreuder (Eds.), *Idioms: Structural and Psychological Perspectives* (pp. 253–271). Hillsdale, NJ: LEA.

Searle, J. (1979). Metaphor. In A. Ortony (Ed.), *Metaphor and Thought* (pp. 92–123). New York: Cambridge University Press.

Searle, J. (1993). Metaphor. In A. Ortony (Ed.), *Metaphor and Thought (2d Ed.)* (pp. 83–111). Cambridge: Cambridge University Press.

Shinjo, M., & Myers, J. (1987). The role of context in metaphor comprehension. *Journal of Memory and Language, 26*, 226–241.

Shinoff, P. (1987). Demjanjuk war-crimes tribunal strikes deep fear among Jews. *San Francisco Examiner*, June 14, p. A8.

Simpson, G. B., & Kang, H. (1994). Inhibitory processes in recognition of homograph meanings. In D. Dagenbach and T. H. Carr (Eds.), *Inhibitory Processes in Attention, Memory and Language* (pp. 359–382). San Diego: Academic Press.

Simpson, G. B., & Krueger, M. A. (1991). Selective access of homograph meanings in sentence context. *Journal of Memory and Language, 30*, 627–643.

Smith, E. E., Osherson, D. N., Rips, L. J., & Keane, M. (1988). Combining prototypes: A selective modification model. *Cognitive Science, 12*, 485–527.

Soskice, J. (1990). *Metaphor and Religious Thought*. Oxford: Clarendon.

Steen, G. (1992). Literary and nonliterary aspects of metaphor. *Poetics Today, 13*, 687–704.

Steen, G. (1994). *Understanding Metaphor in Literature*. London: Longman Group.

Stengel, E. (1939). On learning a new language. *International Journal of Psycho-Analysis, 20*, 471–479.

Stern, J. (2000). *Metaphor in Context*. Cambridge, MA: Bradford/MIT Press.

Stroop, J. R. (1935). Studies of interference in serial verbal reactions. *Journal of Experimental Psychology, 18*, 643–662.

Suppalla, T. (1986). The classifier system in American Sign Language. In C. Craig (Ed.), *Noun Classes and Categorization* (pp. 181–214). Amsterdam/Philadelphia: John Benjamins.

Swinney, D., & Cutler, A. (1979). The access and processing of idiomatic expressions. *Journal of Verbal Learning and Verbal Behavior, 18*, 523–534.

Tabossi, P., & Cacciari, C. (1988). Context effects in the comprehension of idioms. In *Proceedings of the Tenth Annual Conference of the Cognitive Science Society* (pp. 90–96). Hillsdale, NJ: LEA.

Tabossi, P., & Zardon, F. (1993). The activation of idiomatic meaning in spoken language comprehension. In C. Cacciari & P. Tabossi (Eds.), *Idioms: Processing, Structure, and Interpretation* (pp. 145–163). Hillsdale, NJ: LEA.

Tabossi, P., & Zardon, F. (1995). The activation of idiomatic meaning. In M. Everaert, E. van den Linden, A. Schenk, & R. Schreuder (Eds.), *Idioms: Structural and Psychological Perspectives* (pp. 273–282). Hillsdale, NJ: LEA.

Talmy, L. (1996). Fictive motion in language and "ception." In P. Bloom and M. A. Peterson (Eds.), *Language and Space. Language, Speech, and Communication* (pp. 211–276). Cambridge, MA: MIT Press.

Tannenhaus, M. K., Spivey-Knowlton, M. J., Eberhard, K. M., & Sedivy, J. C. (1995). Integration of visual and linguistic information in spoken language comprehension. *Science, 268*, 1632–1634.

Tannenhaus, M. K., Spivey-Knowlton, M. J., Eberhard, K. M., & Sedivy, J. C. (1996). Using eye movements to study spoken language comprehension: Evidence for visually mediated incremental interpretation. In T. Inui and J. L. McClelland (Eds.), *Attention and Performance 16: Information Integration in Perception and Communication* (pp. 457–478). Cambridge, MA: MIT Press.

Torreano, L. (1997). *Understanding Metaphorical Use of Verbs*. Unpublished doctoral dissertation, Princeton University.

Tourangeau, R., and Sternberg, R. J. (1981). Aptness in metaphor. *Cognitive Psychology, 13*, 27–55.

Trager, G. L. (1936–1939). "Cottonwood-Tree": A south-western linguistic trait. *International Journal of American Linguistics, 9*, 117–118.

Turner, M. (1987). *Death Is the Mother of Beauty*. Chicago: University of Chicago Press.

Turner, M. (1991). *Reading Minds: The Study of English in the Age of Cognitive Science*. Princeton, NJ: Princeton University Press.

Tversky, A. (1977). Features of similarity. *Psychological Review, 85*, 327–352.

Tversky, B., & Hemenway, K. (1984). Objects, parts, and categories. *Journal of Experimental Psychology: General, 113*, 169–193.

Van de Voort, M. E. C., & Vonk, W. (1995). You don't die immediately when you kick an empty bucket: A processing view on semantic and syntactic characteristics of idioms. In M. Everaert, and E. van der Linden (Eds.), *Idioms: Structural and Psychological Perspectives* (pp. 283–299). Hillsdale, NJ: Erlbaum.

Wasow, T., Sag, I., & Nunberg, G. (1983). Idioms: An interim report. In S. Hattori & K. Inoue (Eds.), *Proceedings of the 13th International Congress of Linguistics.* Tokyo: CIPL.

Way, E. C. (1991). *Knowledge Representation and Metaphor.* Dordrecht, The Netherlands: Kluwer Academic.

Webster's Dictionary of English Usage. Springfield, MA: Merriam-Webster.

Wechsler, D. (1958). *The Measurement and Appraisal of Adult Intelligence* (4th Ed.). Baltimore, MD: Williams and Wilkins.

Weinrich, U. (1966). Explorations in semantic theory. In T. A. Sebeok (Ed.), *Current Trends in Linguistics*, Vol. 3. The Hague: Mouton.

Whorf, B. L. (1956). *Language, Thought and Reality: Selected Writings of Benjamin Lee Whorf.* New York: Wiley.

Winter, S. L. (1989). Transcendental nonsense, metaphoric reasoning, and the cognitive stakes for law. *University of Pennsylvania Law Review, 137,* 1105–1123.

Winter, S. L. (1992). The meaning of "under color of" law. *Michigan Law Review*, 91, 323–418.

Wisniewski, E. J. (1996). Construal and similarity in conceptual combination. *Journal of Memory and Language, 35,* 434–453.

Wisniewski, E. J. (1997). When concepts combine. *Psychonomic Bulletin and Review, 4,* 167–183.

Wisniewski, E. J. (2000). How do people know where the stripes of a zebra clam go? Comment on Estes & Glucksberg. *Memory and Cognition,* 28, 35–38.

Wisniewski, E. J., & Markman, A. B. (1993). The role of structural alignment in conceptual combination. In *Proceedings of the Fifteenth Annual Conference of the Cognitive Science Society* (pp. 1083–1086). Hillsdale, NJ: Erlbaum.

Wolff, P., & Gentner, D. (1992). The time course of metaphor comprehension. In *Proceedings of the Fourteenth Annual Conference of the Cognitive Science Society,* (pp. 504–509), Hillsdale, NJ: Erlbaum.

Name Index

Aaron, D., 106
Agar, M., 87, 88
Albritton, D. W., 91, 102
Anderson, J. M., 18, 102
Antos, S., 76
Aristotle, 4, 27
Austin, J., 109

Barnes, K., 89
Barsalou, L., 40–44, 48
Battig, W. F., 113
Bell, S. M., 76, 110
Bellugi, U., 39, 43
Bennett, D. C, 102
Besson, M., 20
Bever, T. G., 10
Bierwisch, M., 14, 90
Black, M., 27, 36, 113
Blasko, D. G., 19, 20
Bly, B., 95–97
Boatner, M. T., 97
Bobrow, S. A., 76, 110
Bolton, J. L ., 73
Bookin, H. A., 21
Boroditsky, L., 102
Boronat, C. B., 103
Bowdle, B. F., 37, 104, 110
Brown, M. E., 101
Brown, R., 6, 42, 75,111
Burke, K., 52

Cacciari, C., 21, 71, 73, 76, 78, 79, 81, 114
Camac M., 34, 36
Caramazza, A., 14
Carbonell, J. G., 91
Carroll, P., 18
Catford, J. C., 87, 114
Chukovsky, K., 110
Clark, H. H, 5, 10, 17, 21, 31, 34, 35, 90, 102–103,109
Cohen, B., 60
Connine, C. M., 19, 20
Craig, C., 39
Cruse, D. A., 83
Cutler, A., 68, 76, 77
Cutting, C., 73, 74, 81, 82

Dascal, V., 27
Davidson, D., 8, 80
Denny, J. P., 39
Donne, J., 47
Dubois, J., 109

Eberhard, K. M., 17
Edelin, F., 109
Elman, J. L., 71
Engel, M., 87
Ernst, T., 114
Estes, Z., 60, 62

Subject Index

Abstraction, levels of, 38–43, 54, 64–66, 105

Alignment: structural, 36–37, 60, 91, 113; of topic and vehicle, 54, 60–61

Allusion, 75

Ambiguity: of idioms, 95–98; lexical, 17, 20; of metaphor vehicles, 55–63, 105–106

Analogy, 4

Anthropology, 4, 92

Aptness, 48–50; and proto typicality, 49

Attribution, property, 36, 47, 99–100

Automaticity, of comprehension, 10–11; of metaphor comprehension, 21–28, 110

Category, creation of, 43, 44, 99

Categories: attributive, 41–44, basic level, 40, 42; functional, 42–44, 48; graded, 43; hierarchical, 42–43; metaphoric, 41, 42, 99–100; naming, 38–42

Categorization, levels of, 5, 42, 111

Class inclusion, 44, 99–100; implicit, 45; negation of, 47

Combination, conceptual, 28, 53, 59–63

Comparison, 30, 54, 60; metaphoric, 32–33;

Compositionality, of idioms, 69, 72

Comprehensibility, metaphor, 48

Concepts: metaphoric representation of, 92–98; natural kind, 105

Connectives, logical, 13–14

Constraint: attributional, 54, 56; topic, 55–63

Construction, property, 59

Context, 8, 22–23

Context-dependence, 12, 17–19,

Contrast model (of similarity), 30–33

Conversation, maxims of, 9

Cooperative principle, 5, 9, 47

Decoding, linguistic, 11, 16, 21, 110

Deviance, semantic, 45, 49

Differences, alignable, 60

Dimensions: for attribution, 53, 98; relevance of, 53

Expressions, fixed, 68

Features: introduction, 35, 37; matching, 30–36; salience, 30–36; selection, 30, 34–37

Flexibility: semantic, 73, 81–83; syntactic, 69, 73, 81–83